Awaken to the Brand New You

The Path to Reinventing Oneself

Luis Soto Jr

BALBOA PRESS
A DIVISION OF HAY HOUSE

Copyright © 2014 Luis Soto Jr.

All rights reserved. No part of this book may be used or reproduced by any means, graphic, electronic, or mechanical, including photocopying, recording, taping or by any information storage retrieval system without the written permission of the publisher except in the case of brief quotations embodied in critical articles and reviews.

Used Prayer for Protection with permission of Unity, www.unity.org.

Balboa Press books may be ordered through booksellers or by contacting:

Balboa Press
A Division of Hay House
1663 Liberty Drive
Bloomington, IN 47403
www.balboapress.com
1 (877) 407-4847

Because of the dynamic nature of the Internet, any web addresses or links contained in this book may have changed since publication and may no longer be valid. The views expressed in this work are solely those of the author and do not necessarily reflect the views of the publisher, and the publisher hereby disclaims any responsibility for them.

The author of this book does not dispense medical advice or prescribe the use of any technique as a form of treatment for physical, emotional, or medical problems without the advice of a physician, either directly or indirectly. The intent of the author is only to offer information of a general nature to help you in your quest for emotional and spiritual well-being. In the event you use any of the information in this book for yourself, which is your constitutional right, the author and the publisher assume no responsibility for your actions.

Any people depicted in stock imagery provided by Thinkstock are models, and such images are being used for illustrative purposes only.
Certain stock imagery © Thinkstock.

Printed in the United States of America.

ISBN: 978-1-4525-1453-6 (sc)
ISBN: 978-1-4525-1451-2 (hc)
ISBN: 978-1-4525-1452-9 (e)

Library of Congress Control Number: 2014908510

Balboa Press rev. date: 10/28/2014

Contents

Acknowledgements..vii
Foreword..xi
Preface..xv
Introduction..xvii

Part 1 The Evolution of a Broken Boy 1
   Chapter 1   My Childhood...3
   Chapter 2   A Man Trying to Make Sense Out of Life 13
   Chapter 3   The Internal Earthquake..............................23

Part 2 Victimhood: Where the Journey Begins 27
   Chapter 4   Overcoming Addictions................................29
   Chapter 5   My Belief in God 35
   Chapter 6   Confronted by My Past.................................41

Part 3 The Light Is Both Near and Far from You.......47
   Chapter 7   The Road to Recovery.................................49
   Chapter 8   The Will to Persevere 58
   Chapter 9   Putting All the Pieces Together....................64

Part 4 Embracing Solitude 69
   Chapter 10   The Gift of Starting All Over Again 71
   Chapter 11   The Five Stages of Awakening.....................78
   Chapter 12   Love, Forgiveness, and Gratitude 89

Conclusion...95
Personal Notes..103
References..107

"There are only two mistakes one can make along the road to truth: not going all the way and not starting."

- Buddha

Acknowledgements

I want to acknowledge all the people that God sent my way to help me write and publish this book. The universe is always beckoning at our call when we are ready to play a big game in life. I could not have completed this project without the help of these angels that played a significant role in writing my book. First and foremost, I acknowledge the omnipresence that has transform my life and given me a second chance to do things right. The spirit of God is eternal and I surrender the whole process to infinite intelligence to manifest this book in your hands.

Thank you Stephanie Fiallo and Gary Salvit for providing a space and platform for me to co-create with the rest of the mastermind group of 2013 to start the process of writing my book. I appreciate your support, love, time and patience with me when the book was only a thought, a desire that through the support of the Master Mind group became a manifestation. I am deeply grateful for your generous contribution towards me and my book. I love you!

Thank you Balboa Press team for providing me the tools, structure, support, love and patience working with me diligently to finish my book. I highly recommend anyone who is thinking about writing their story to work with Balboa Press, Exceptional Professionalism and kindness to help you self-publish your book.

Thank you Dr. Reverend Bessie Duncan for your spiritual mentorship, guidance, prayers and support with helping me through my journey to awaken my Christ Mind consciousness. I love my Unity Church of Christ in Teaneck NJ congregation. I am thankful for my spiritual family for always being there and never judging me with my mistakes while I was in the process to awaken to the brand new me. I love my Unity church!

Thank you Coach Dave Buck and Coach Dianna Stull and the rest of the Coachville community for providing the guidance, tools, support and enthusiasm to persevere with completing my book. I love Coachville and all the wonderful transformation that I received becoming the person I am today. Thank you!

Thank you Joan Hermann and for your support with the creation of my book. I appreciate your friendship and support with all the advice and time you gave me unconditionally. Thank you!

Thank you Caryn Chow for being an example of light and victory. You are truly a guiding light to me and your friends and family. May God continue to bless you abundantly!

Thank you Amy Garcia for your support in editing my book. I appreciate your writing talent and I'm grateful God sent you to help me finish my book. Wishing you much success and prosperity in all areas of your life.

Thank you Peter Brash for taking time out of your busy schedule and mentoring me to start writing my ideas on paper.

You truly gave me great suggestions on how to overcome my writer's block and how to allow my genius to express itself on paper.

Wishing you much success and prosperity in all your endeavors.

Thank you to all my friends and family that have always loved me unconditionally.

And we always save the best for last. I want to thank my soul mate for her generosity of spirit, commitment to our partnership and the completion of my book. There are no words to describe the love, admiration and respect I have for you, my love. I honor your presence and I thank God for giving me the best gift I could ever imagine. I love you till eternity, Amor.

God bless you!

"Our greatest glory is not in never falling, but in getting up every time we do."

- Confucius
Chinese philosopher & reformer
(551 BC - 479 BC)

Foreword

What does it mean to be awake?
What is the path to reinventing oneself!
How does someone start the process of becoming awake?
These are the questions that make our soul realign with our purpose in life.

Picture yourself living your life as mundane as can be. All of a sudden, your inner voice asks you to start doing something new. Fears come when we decide to play a bigger game than the one we are playing now. Life is fascinating! There are many twists and turns that we take to find ourselves. The journey begins when we feel a deeper calling that is congruent with our core beliefs and values. Before that can happen to us, we must be willing to release our secret that has kept us in captivity all this time.

A secret is something that as kids, we would hide from each other. The only problem is, as we grow up and become adults, those same secrets start to control and dictate our choices and actions that lead us to never waking up from our dormant sleep of existence. The more unconscious we are about our secrets, the harder it will be to fully manifest our desires. What is required for us to wake up and live a purposeful life?

1. The first step is to have the willingness to grow from who you were to who you want to become…
2. Have the openness to experiment and try something new.
3. Nurture an attitude of gratitude for everything that you have in your life.
4. Stop making excuses and take full responsibility for everything that has transpired in your life.
5. Be willing to forgive yourself and others for all the mistakes of your past.
6. Start the process of transformation by saying YES I CAN to the universe!
7. Live life from a place of play versus fear of the unknown.
8. Begin to share your vision with the world of your perfect life.
9. Bathe in the present moment and relish in the now!
10. Try your best and don't hold back from giving your all.

The path to awaken to the brand new you takes courage, resilience, patience, love for yourself, and the determination to live your life now!

Many of us have a difficult time following our bliss because the past continues to revisit us everywhere we go. As we journey into the unknown, we come across fears and disbeliefs that continue to resurface in our lives. The more we move forward in breaking through the resistance of fear, the easier it will be to awaken to the brand new you.

The time has come to break free from the shell that has kept you quiet and safe. No more will you shy away from opportunities that will help you grow and expand in your consciousness. This is your season to shine your light and give birth to your ideas and image of who you were born to be.

The process of becoming begins the moment you surrender to yourself and the universe. Allow yourself to be intuitively guided by spirit and not the ego. Live your life now! Take ownership of your magnificence and bathe in the power of your being.

The world is waiting for you to unleash your gifts and talents for massive contribution. "Walk your walk and talk your talk." Those are the steps for you to live in integrity and congruency to whom you really are. You are a beacon of light. God took great pride and joy to create you just the way you are. If your upbringing was horrific and traumatic, it does not take away the value that you are a human being. You matter, we all matter. Everyone on this planet matters and we are here to learn from each other and grow spiritually into whom we are becoming.

Before the butterfly is fully grown, there has to be a continuous metamorphosis that evolves from an egg, to a caterpillar then a chrysalis into a beautiful, radiant, vibrant butterfly. Even though the life span of a butterfly could be a week or a year, this marvelous creature spreads its wings and lives in the present moment. The incredible stages of transformation requires determination and a knowing of who it was born to be.

Think about your life and all the changes that you have been through?

How many times did you interfere with the growing stages of your life? Before we can emerge into our brand new you, there must be a period of gestation to form and mature the consciousness into existence. Trust the process that you are going through right now. Understand and know that all is always in divine order. It is up to us to realign ourselves with the order of the universe to see and witness the magic and miracles taking place in our lives.

As we get ready to say good bye to winter and embrace the spring, allow yourself to release what no longer serves you and welcome your new skin of spiritual maturity.

Make a list of 10 things that you will give away from your past. Once you create that void, the universe will then respond with more prosperity and abundance to satisfy and fulfill your need. Also, think about what negative behavior and habits you are committed to releasing as well. The past no longer exists in your new awareness of being.

Take heart my spiritual warrior and continue on the road less traveled. The uncertainty will bring you magic, excitement and unprecedented opportunity to keep your journey fun and enjoyable. Live your best life today and don't look back!

You are loved, beloved. May the spirit of God shine upon you!

Namaste,
Luis Soto Jr.
Transformational Life Coach

Preface

The book you are holding in your hands has tremendous power, light, and truth. I wrote this book for all who have experienced any form of childhood abuse: physical, verbal, mental, and sexual. If you were bullied, ridiculed, or made to feel like you were a mistake when you were born, then this book will set you free from your tormented past. This is the story of a boy who, despite the trauma, sexual abuse, and rejection he received while growing up, rose to the occasion and became an independent, mature, confident man.

Before we go any further into my story, I must tell you that my intent for writing this book is to let you know that I do not regret my past. I have forgiven everyone who has harmed me in any way, intentionally or unintentionally. My greatest gift has come from all my adversity, pain, struggle, and desperation to make sense of my purpose in life. I have contemplated and procrastinated writing this book because it deals with a great deal of shame, guilt, hurt, and pain from my past. In order for my past to have validation, I offer myself to the reader, as you will discover insights, breakthroughs, and aha moments that will lead you to awaken the brand-new you.

"Take the first step in faith, you don't have to see the whole staircase, just take the first step."

- Dr. Martin Luther King, Jr.

Introduction

This book is a guide for making amends with your past and celebrating and Awakening the Brand-New You. My story is a platform for love, forgiveness, and gratitude, which enables you to free yourself from your past hurts and reclaim your true essence. Whatever form of abuse you witnessed or personally experienced and endured, please know that all was in divine order. That experience set the stage for you to do your greatest work here on this planet. There are no accidents nor bad luck in life; there are only different perspectives on what happened and the meaning and beliefs we create from those experiences. Until now, your past hurts or the injustices done to you may have enslaved you. Today, we set ourselves free from our past and create the path to reawaken yourself.

Embrace my story, and look at where you are currently stuck in your life. I will provide a map on how to move from victim to warrior. You are not alone; the universe adores and wants you to win. Start loving yourself today, and become fully responsible for everything that has transpired in your life. That will provide you with tremendous freedom to create a new world of possibilities. We were all born to be great. Our greatest gift lives within us. Now is the time to journey within and reclaim our treasure. The beauty of who you are is waiting for your command. Take ownership of your gifts and talents, and allow yourself to share the magnificence of your being.

There is no more time to waste. You must act now. Today. Life happens in the present moment. With every step you take toward awakening to the brand-new you, the universe will provide the way to open the doors of opportunity for you. My friend and spiritual seeker, I welcome you to the path of reinventing oneself. Congratulations on taking the first step to your new and wonderful life.

Part One

The Evolution of a Broken Boy

"The secret of change is to focus all of your energy, not on fighting the old, but on building the new."

- Socrates

Chapter 1

My Childhood

Growing up in Washington Heights in the early seventies and eighties was a very difficult time for me. When I was in the third grade, I was afflicted with rheumatic fever, a severe disease characterized by painful inflammation of the joints and damage to the heart valves. I remember going to the hospital for the first time and receiving my first vaccine in my thigh that made me sore for a couple of days. The rheumatic fever landed me in the hospital for a couple of months, and as a result, I was retained in school and placed in special class because my reading was not up to par with my peers.

I openly and transparently share my story with you, so that something might resonate with you at any moment. You may stop and ask yourself, "How is this story relevant in my life today?" Remember, there is no shame from your past, only gems and blessings that will set you free from where you currently are in your journey to awaken to the brand-new you.

I was a skinny, timid, and withdrawn little boy who had no idea about what life was about. I was literally clueless as to why I was alive. I had zero confidence and low self-esteem. I became a victim of bullying because I was not taught how to defend myself. Even though I had friends around, there was still something bothering me inside that I couldn't make sense of at the time. As I write, share, and reveal my past to you, think back to when you were a kid and allow the emotions of the past to resurface to your conscious mind. What past experiences as a child did you ignore that has created problems in your life today? *For example, you may ask yourself "…",* as I continue to share my story of transformation with you. I was not aware of what was lurking in the darkness that created all my struggles and sadness in my life. Being a kid and not knowing the facts of life can create confusion early on as you start to develop friendships with friends and family. Children are playful, trusting, and require a great deal of affection from their parents and family members. It is easy to see how a child is misled to inappropriate relationships that confuse their understanding of love and intimacy. This is exactly what happened to me in my early childhood years.

Growing up without a big brother was something difficult for me. My grandparents in Puerto Rico were raising my big brother, and we only were able to see him about once every couple of years. Once, my brother came to visit during the summer; we had so much fun playing outside in the park throwing Frisbee, playing tag, and enjoying each other's company.

Unfortunately, this brotherly relationship was not what I had been signed up for. My mother would take us to PR occasionally to visit our grandparents, and we would see my older brother there as well. At the time, I was around six years old. It is hard to know exactly how old I was because these hurtful emotions have been stored away for such a long time in an effort to conceal my past, hide my pain, and protect my family from ever knowing the truth about my sexual abuse.

My brother, who was five years my senior, physically molested me in the bathroom. I was not aware of what was happening when he came from behind and penetrated me. He told me that this was a game called "horsey." Out of love for my brother, I went along, believing him and trusting that it was okay to be physical with your sibling in such a way.

This day changed my life forever. I must tell you that this experience led to a life filled with alcohol, sex, codependent relationships, and emotional eating. I was tormented, bullied, and beat on because my self-esteem was nonexistent. I was emotionally unstable, depressed, sad, shy, withdrawn, and dead inside.

My salvation came from working out every day at the age of 17. I vividly recall the day that I looked at myself in the mirror and was disgusted by the way my body looked. My stomach was protruding out like a beach ball, and I vowed to never let that happen to me again. That was one of the reasons why I became a personal fitness trainer. I wanted to help people change their physical health and feel better about themselves.

I had gained thirty-five pounds within three years due to a lack of exercise. I decided to go on a ham and cheese, no mayo diet. I lost the thirty-five pounds in five weeks. This started me on a journey to health, wellness and fitness, but the underlying sexual abuse and hurt from my past would reverberate throughout my life.

By no means do I, as a health, fitness, and wellness professional, recommend this extreme, excessive, and destructive way to lose weight. I only implemented this weight loss regimen to cope and escape from my pain. The healthy way to losing weight is with a program that incorporates exercise, nutrition, and a balance of mind, body, and spirit activities to keep you grounded and centered with your body. Yoga, meditation, and Tai Chi are wonderful tools to nurture both your mind and spirit.

* * *

There are different types of child abuse:

- **Physical:** When a child is physically beaten to learn discipline
- **Verbal:** When the parent degrades the child with negative beliefs about who he/ she is in the world
- **Mental:** When the child is emotionally manipulated, making the child feel like it is his/ her fault for the abuse
- **Sexual:** When a family member, guardian, or authority figure takes advantage of the child's innocence for their selfish pleasure

All of these types of child abuse I mentioned are commonplace in today's society and it's getting worse. No one is speaking out about the long-term negative and destructive effects this has on a child, let alone preparing him/ her to live mediocre lives because of their low self-esteem and lack of love for him/ herself. This book is my story with many facets- past, present and future. I want to create awareness around the term "child abuse." What does that really mean? *Child abuse. (n.d.) In child Abuse Definitions, Retrieved August 23, 2014, from http://www.childhelp.org/page/-pdfs/Child-Abuse-Definitions.pdf.*

Let's take neglect for starters. It's childhood abuse:

- When unruly parents fight, scream, and disrespect each other in front of their child.
- When parents do not provide the right amount of love, care, and affection and are emotionally withdrawn and distant from their kids.
- When a child is left alone under the supervision of an adult, parent, or guardian and there is inappropriate touching to a child's private parts.

- When a parent or adult is speaking negatively to a child, reinforcing that he/she is stupid and will never make a life for him/ herself.

I personally believe most people think that childhood abuse is only when a child is beaten or molested. The ugly truth about this destructive epidemic is that this type of abuse is caused by parents and adults who don't know how to manage their own emotions, so they take it out on their kids.

Please keep this in mind. A child is vulnerable to what you have him/her do, teaching him the difference between right and wrong. A child is not there to be your punching bag or venting outlet. Your behaviors and actions are influencing these young kids all the time. The long-term effect that this type of abuse has on a child is devastating.

A child's upbringing creates their self-confidence and self-worth. If he/she were neglected, beaten, and emotionally tortured every time he/she made a mistake, think about their emotions for once. A child's nervous system is not fully developed, and he/she doesn't have the understanding or awareness on why he is always being punished. So their conclusion is typically, "I'm not good enough," or "I'm stupid, and nobody loves me." These beliefs then turn into reality when the child is an adult and has a hard time maintaining a healthy relationship, not living up to their full potential, and coping with substance abuse problems.

When anyone, especially a family member, sexually molests a child, the pain that lives inside of him starts to grow into this poisonous limited self- belief:

- "You are not enough."
- "No one loves you."
- "You are accountable."

A person's mind convinces itself that it was his/ her fault; therefore, he deserves the abuse. Shame and guilt color a person's life, and he can't do anything in that moment; it takes time to break the cycle of thought. These types of beliefs will destroy anything good a person has in their life because the underlying theme of his/ her life is, "I'm not good enough to love, and I'm not enough." So the person starts hurting and pushing people away before people hurt him.

Then on top of all that mental garbage the person deals with on a daily basis in their head and spirit, society places judgment on him because he/ she was molested and they don't know how to treat or deal with him. The world makes it seem like the person asked to be sexually abused. This is one of the reasons why people decide to keep the secret about their abuse- so no one would look at them like there is a defect with him.

That nonsense stops now. I wrote this book so people can set themselves free from their secrets of the past. It does not matter what happened to you. What matters now is that you start the process of liberating yourself from the darkness and go into the light. I hope and pray that people will read my story and come out of the closet of denial and start living their truth of who they really are. If you need help then, "Ask and it shall be given you; seek and ye shall find; knock, and it shall be opened unto you"). (Matt. 7:7–11) New living Translation. Statistically, one in six boys before the age of sixteen has had a childhood history of sexual abuse before the period ("Survivors," 2014).

Here's the big truth for everyone reading my book. My story is a platform for anyone who has experienced any sexual abuse to come forward and set yourself free from your past hurts and mistakes in your life. Jesus said, "Then you will know the truth, and the truth will set you free" (John 8:32).

The more a person tries to conceal his/ her secret about abuse, the more tortured their life will be. When you don't have to suppress your emotions and pretend to be someone you are not, now you start living your truth.

No more hiding or denying that you were a victim of sexual abuse. This is the moment to turn this hurt into your greatest blessing. Share your experience with someone today, and start the process of love, forgiveness, and gratitude in your life. Use this book as your guiding light to break free from the demons in your past. You are no longer a victim of your past circumstances if you choose not to be.

Today, you take your power back and reclaim your innocence. There is nothing to be ashamed of from your past. This book is about creating awareness for everyone involved in your life. Remember, if they knew better, they would have done better.

That was then, and this is now. I believe there comes a time when we all must be responsible and hold each other accountable for our actions. Whether they were right or wrong, it does not really matter in the big picture because that's how we learn, grow, and evolve in our consciousness to be the best self we can be. Mistakes will be made along our path toward enlightenment. Expect and embrace them. That's how we become the manifestation of spirit in our own life.

Last year has left its mark; now this is the year for you to become fully alive with your life. Start by reading my book and writing in your journal every day. Share your secret with someone you trust, and let that poison out slowly. This process will start you living your truth and honoring your divine self again. You owe it to yourself and the world to live your truth. I commend your bravery of coming out and releasing the baggage of your past. On this next page, write down your secret with me. This book will help you Awaken the Brand-New You. Thank you for trusting my guidance on unraveling your magnificence.

Share your secret with me, and set yourself free from your past. I'm here for you. Remember, you are beautiful and God loves you.

Luis Soto Jr

SHARE YOUR SECRET WITH ME.

*   *   *

Thank you for trusting me with this exercise. If you really went for it, you should feel lighter all over your body now. I know that writing down your secret brought memories you'd rather not face, but in order to set yourself free from your past, this type of honesty, willingness, and courage is required to experience love, forgiveness, and gratitude in your heart and mind. If you experience tears for the first time, I'm glad, but if you didn't, then maybe you are still closed from allowing the painful emotions to come to the surface of your conscious mind. This process is called "chemicalization," which is when you are committed to starting something new and your new intentions confront your old negative beliefs, behaviors, and habits. Before the period "(Truth Unity,n.d)" If this is the first time being honest with yourself, then you are coming up against all those years of confinement, secrecy, guilt, and shame from your past.

This process is purifying your mind, body, and spirit to live a new idea and a new way of being (living your truth). Expect meltdowns, both emotional and physical. It may feel like you were lost in a deep, thick fog and all of a sudden there was light. This turbulence and confusion is part of the process of going deeper into your spiritual unfoldment. Don't fight the process. Allow all the toxins to be flushed out of your body and mind.

Make sure to drink plenty of water to replenish all the energy lost in the cleansing process. You will now start being tested to move forward with your new belief of who you are becoming. Remember, you are a child of God. You have the magnificence inside of you to create a new and wonderful life. Take hold, my spiritual seeker of truth, and trust your faith in God. Stay grounded in prayer and meditation, and keep writing in your journal. There is no turning back now. From here, there's only light, awareness, and your truth leading the way to the brand-new you. Express your divinity and stay true to whom you were born to be. The power and light of the magnificence exist in your being. Trust the divine nature of your soul and relish in the miracle of redemption and transformation in your life. Peace be with you always. Namaste

Recite the prayer of protection by James Dillet Freeman to stay grounded in God.

> *The light of God surrounds us;*
> *The love of God enfolds us*
> *The power of God protects us;*
> *The presence of God watches over us;*
> *Wherever we are, God is and all is well.*
> *Wherever you are, God is and all is well.*
> *Wherever I am, God is and all is well.*
> *And so it is!*
> *Amen.*

Chapter 2

A Man Trying to Make Sense Out of Life

When a boy is molested at a young age, the aftermath of the abuse interferes with the child's developmental stages into his adolescent and adult years. This young boy turns into a man who still feels like he's six years old. This traumatic experience takes hold of the young man trying his best to deal with life's challenges every day of his life. No matter how much the person is in denial from the abuse, the result in his life reigns over logic and reasoning. One of the hardest things this man tries to do is erase the experience from his mind.

Interestingly, the abuse became relevant when I was in therapy in my early thirties. Still then, the emotions were buried so deep inside of me that I managed to cover it up with distractions and drama with all the unwise choices I was making in my life.

The guilt comes from feeling responsible for the abuse. These types of emotions are insidious to your mind and consciousness. The guilt starts to build momentum in your mind and spirit, and the ego starts to have a field day with your addictions of alcohol, sex, and emotional eating. I was not aware that this negative tag team—guilt and shame—was controlling my life until my last therapist pointed it out to me. But I was too weak inside to prevent these strong emotions from overtaking my life. It did not matter how many visits to the therapist's office I'd made in a month. The underlying issue was guilt and shame. Even having the awareness did not break the chains of my past.

I have realized now that, in order to break the negative pull, we must be willing to let go of our story for good. My past continued to recirculate in my life because of the unwillingness to let it go. We could remain victims of our circumstances as long as the world- and we ourselves- validate our victim story. What I have come to realize is that my story is not original. Other people had it worse than I did. But the difference is that they surrendered their victim story to a higher power like I did. Now I see how my sexual abuse experience has provided me the platform to do my transformative work on this planet. This has become my blueprint to serve humanity in a powerful way. Now is your turn to do the same. Welcome, truth seeker, to the brand-new you.

Once I really started to pay attention to all my choices that were leading me into drama, I knew I had to do a great deal of inner work within myself. The ego started to reveal its ugly head when I went to my first therapy session after breaking off a relationship I was in for three years. Again, I was not aware of how buried the abuse with my brother was inside of me. We started addressing other issues like family, relationships, and so forth. Still, I had no idea that the sexual abuse with my brother was an ongoing problem for me. I worked with the therapist for a couple months, and then it was time to implement the therapy in my life.

Keep in mind that, even though I went to a therapist, I was not open to receiving guidance from anyone. My ego was in charge, and I was very arrogant, judgmental, and critical with everyone in my circle of friends and family. That's what happens when you have no awareness of your behavior and how this hurt and abuse could keep you locked up in your mind for good.

My personal training business started to thrive, and I found myself making lots of money in my late twenties and early thirties. The attention I was receiving from everyone was a bit overwhelming, to say the least. Clients were signing up left and right. I was single and dating lots of girls, and I was staying out partying like a rock star—drinking, spending lots of money, and really living life big time.

In truth, I was so alone inside me that I disguised it by staying in amazing shape and always having company with me every night. I would get home around three or four in the morning on the weekdays, drunk and numb about the abuse. I thought I was king, so I lavished myself with great clothes, restaurants, and weekend trips, but still I managed to be in debt with all the money I was making from my lucrative personal-training business. I share my story with you openly so you can see your life and the way the past might have influenced you in a negative way.

As you can imagine, I put on extra weight pretty quickly despite working out five times a week. My going out every night of the week was becoming very excessive and out of control. I found myself falling into the NYC lifestyle of socially drinking, hooking up, and being careless with my actions. From the perspective of the outside world, it would have seemed I had my life together, but in reality, I was a sad, lonely, scared little boy living inside of a thirty-something year-old man.

When we are abused as kids, that experience is deep in our subconscious mind where all our beliefs, behaviors, and habits exist. I always made sure I had company around me to prevent the truth from revealing itself to me. This behavior went on for a couple years, and I decided it was time to start something new.

I went back to my therapist and told him that I was feeling depressed and sad all the time. He evaluated me to see if I were suffering from chronic depression before recommending me to see a psychiatrist. The result showed that I suffered from mild depression so we discussed a natural way of dealing with the problem. He mentioned an herb called St. John's wort, an alternative, natural treatment for depression. That really made me happy because I did not want to use drugs for my mental condition. This would help me with my depression, and it was natural.

I started taking St. John's wort right away, just like my therapist recommended, for a couple months. In the meantime, I wanted to start healing myself from depression and alcohol by starting a meditation practice. I was determined to get off the medication by curing myself with the meditation. Every day, I would commit to sitting on my cushion for five to ten minutes, sometimes meditating twice a day.

I started noticing changes with my attitude and depression, and I slowly started backing off from the St. John's wort. I originally started with the high doses of three pills a day. As my belief in myself grew, so did my meditation practice to thirty to sixty minutes a day. I remember that defining day when I looked at myself in the mirror and finally got off the medication. I knew that, in order to be healed, I had to stand in faith and believe I was healed from my depression. That was the day that I replaced drugs with meditation. Until this day, my meditation has been my natural drug for the past eight years, and I attribute my sobriety to this transformative tool for awakening and transformation of oneself.

Despite my freedom from depression, I was still deep in pain with my sexual abuse. I decided to get involved with someone and start a family, hoping that would help heal my pain from my childhood past. But my unresolved sexual abuse issue was deeply ingrained in my soul that I destroyed any relationship that came my way. That resulted in a divorce that landed me back at my parents' home. I was embarrassed and down on myself. I was broken and sad about why my life was not working out for me.

One day, I was out riding my Vespa along the Palisades Highway, crying and feeling emotionally disturbed with my life. I really was in no condition to be riding my bike when my emotions were so raw and open as they were on that transformative day of fate. I was getting ready to get off the exit toward my parents' home when, all of a sudden, I changed my mind and turned the opposite way toward the oncoming traffic of cars moving at least fifty to sixty miles an hour. Knowing I just made a huge mistake with my judgment, I braced myself for the blow and force of this car that had no choice but to hit me, and I flew off the bike onto the ground, shaken and disoriented from my fall. Immediately within seconds, the person who hit my bike was by my side with police and EMTs. The paramedics took me to the hospital to make sure everything was okay with me.

When I woke up the next day, my mother drove me to see my chiropractor who was considered a healer by everyone he worked with. Right away, he took X-rays and started praying to God for my healing. The X-rays showed that my sacrum was bruised pretty badly and all the nerves surrounding that area of my spine as well. He recommended I take off a couple weeks from work to heal my body. I called my clients and informed them about my accident and the doctor's order to rest. Everyone was understanding and supportive toward me feeling better and coming back to work.

I asked myself, "What is the blessing behind my accident?" Then instantly, a flash of inspiration and guidance took over my being. Spirit instructed me to go to the basement and start reading a book by Eric Butterworth called *Discover the Power within You*.

Interestingly, I bought that book one year ago when I met a man who told me about Eric Butterworth and his Sunday sermons at Avery Fisher Hall in NYC. We got into a deep conversation about God and spirituality, and I went that week and bought the book, but I had not read the book until this moment because I was not ready to listen to the message. As I say, "The universe is always in divine order. It is up to us to realign ourselves with the order of the universe to receive the guidance and answers we are seeking for our life."

I devoured that book from cover to cover. The energy and inspiration I felt from the book opened my eyes to believing in miracles. From that moment on, every day felt like a blessing. I was grateful that I had this companion to help me see the blessing with my accident. After I finished reading the book, I wanted to know where I could go to get this spiritual nourishment that my soul was yearning for. I went on the computer and found out more about Unity Church of Christ and the location of the nearest one to me. As serendipitous as this can be, a Unity church was ten minutes from my parents' house.

I was so excited to go to service on Sunday and learn more about Unity and its spiritual principles. The day finally came when I walked into my first Unity service, and I instantly knew I found home. I stood up and introduced myself to the congregation, and they received me with open arms and their unity blessing. "Friends and visitors, we love you, we appreciate you, and we behold the Christ in you." That's how many Unity churches welcome guests to the house of God. I knew I found home and it was time to get close to my spiritual roots.

Right away, I became involved with the church—Bible study, book club, meditation ministry, and a candidate for the board of the church. Unity helped me understand more about God and the relationship I had with this omnipresent source of love. Now that

I was on my way toward healing and discovering the divine in me, I decided to give myself a special birthday present by enrolling in the intensive two-hundred-hour course at Kripalu, a center of yoga and health, to become a yoga teacher. The life-changing training I received in Kripalu was transformative.

One night, I was writing on my journal about my day, and all of a sudden, this intense tidal wave of emotions knocked me on the floor, and I started crying hysterically. For the first time in my life, I became present to the sexual abuse from my brother. My intuition told me that I must share this breakthrough information with my class the next day. I went up to my teachers and told them what came up for me last night, and they encouraged and supported me to share my revelation about my sexual abuse from my brother to the group.

As you can imagine, some people were shocked, disturbed, and angry at me for coming out so boldly and sharing my deepest secrets to strangers. I knew that, once I spoke about the abuse, the poison inside of me would start to free my body from the pain. Once I completed my yoga certification, I decided to go back to my original therapist and start working on my issue with my sexual abuse.

My therapist encouraged me to confront my brother so I could put my story to rest. I decided to take my therapist's advice, and I went to Florida to confront my brother about my abuse. My brother was very happy to see me, and we started talking about life and the way things always manage to work out in the end. I kept pushing myself to confront him, but we got into an argument about something else, and my window of opportunity shut down on me. I was upset and annoyed with myself that I couldn't tell him about the sexual abuse.

I went back to my therapist's office, and we talked about forgiveness and the reason it is so important to forgive those who hurt us, consciously or unconsciously. I tried to forgive, but I couldn't do it. My heart was bitter and angry now that I knew about the sexual abuse from my brother. I stopped calling him or receiving his messages. In my eyes, I did not care about my brother's well-being at all. Then after three years of not speaking with him, I finally saw him at a barbecue that we were having for Mother's Day. My brother was not well, he looked very ill, and he couldn't stay up much of the time. He would sleep all day and spend little time with us. I felt sympathy for him, but I still kept my distance from him.

When it was time for him to go home, I told him that I loved him and asked him to please go to the doctor and call me. He told me he would, but he never did. Two weeks after my brother left my mother's home, he passed away. It was too late for him to restore his health back again. After my brother's death, I asked myself, "What would have happened if I had confronted him and we had made amends with the abuse? Would he still be alive today?"

You see, this is a great opportunity to ask yourself, "What grudges am I holding on to from my past?" We never know what is possible if we just forgive and release the poison that is inside of us. Please don't wait until is too late to reconcile your hurt, betrayal, and disappointment about your past. I pray that you find it in your heart to start the process of love, forgiveness, and gratitude in your life and release what no longer serves your highest good. God made us in His image and likeness; therefore, we have the capacity to love unconditionally, forgive wholeheartedly even if it hurts to do, and have the utmost gratitude for our life. Remember, once your time is up, you are no longer in the game of life. Take this moment now and share your deepest sorrow and hurt with me, and we can heal one another. On the next page, write down anything that is in your way of receiving your blessing from God. If you need to forgive someone, then do it. If it was a negative experience that you continue to play over and over in your head then, that stops now. Let's heal each other together, family. Life is too short to waste precious time reliving your past hurts, mistakes, and blunders of the past. Today, you set yourself free from the prison of your mind. God loves you. The universe adores you. Let's make this year the best year ever.

Hi, family, take this page, and write down your hurt so we can heal each other. I believe in you. Namaste.

Take this moment to write down your deepest sorrow and pain so you can heal yourself from your past.

Chapter 3

The Internal Earthquake

Why is it that every time we are about to move forward in our spiritual growth, something intense has to happen to us? It is our intention to expand in consciousness to the point that we call forth "the internal earthquake" to erupt what no longer serves us. When this uncomfortable experience happens to us in our mind, body, and spirit, we think that this experience will last forever. Our emotions are very convincing at times, and we must stay grounded in spirit to rise above the tidal waves of doubt, fear, and confusion. This powerful quote from George Addair sums it up. "Everything that we want is on the other side of fear." Addair, G (2013, Sept24). Cloture Club. Retrieved from http://www.clotureclub.com/2013/09/everything-want-side-fear-george-addair

Think about it. Fear really is a state of mind. It is a state of consciousness that can shift only if we are willing to endure the "internal earthquake inside of us." Before I called Balboa Press, I endured five days of internal earthquake in my soul. I did not want to call and start the process of self-publishing my book. My mind had a field day with me. All my addictions rose to the surface and tried to convince me that my life was upside down.

I went into a mild depression and started eating everything in sight. Plus, I watched excessive television until the long hours of the night. I did not want to work out or eat healthy food. My body, mind, and spirit were craving sweets and junk food that would numb my desires to break through to the other side of fear. It felt like being on a trip to a wonderful destination, and all of a sudden, thunderstorms, sleet, hail, and snow rerouted the trip.

At that crucial moment, I knew that things needed to change in order for me to finish my book. Then from a stroke of luck, I received a call from my client who wanted to work out on Sunday morning. I knew the universe gave me a way out to cross over from fear to possibility. Right after seeing my client, I enrolled in an unlimited yoga membership with Laughing Lotus NYC and bought my Breville juicer to have my green juice every day. Once I started doing yoga three to five days a week and juicing every day, my consciousness shifted, and now you are reading my book.

Right now, you might be experiencing your own internal earthquake that will lead you to your next spiritual awakening to the brand-new you. Remember, this eruption is coming from your desire to expand in your awareness and live your truth. When this disturbance shows up in your mind, embrace it, and allow yourself to go through the process of change, unfoldment, and expansion of your divine self. Our tendency is to fight the change and run away as fast as we can. If we decide to run away from our own internal earthquake, several things can happen:

1. We go back to our comfort zone and lock all the doors and windows from our conscious mind.
2. We have to start the momentum again to build that thrust in our emotions.
3. We are sending a negative message to the universe that we don't need any help and to leave us alone.

The universe and Law of Attraction responds by telling you, "Your wish is my command," and you will continue to attract everything that is not in alignment with your desires and essence of who you are. So really, my dear spiritual seeker of truth, you have no more excuses to run away and not grow into your brand-new you.

Hicks, A. (2014, Aug 1). In an excerpt from a workshop July 8, 2000. Retrieved from http://www.abraham-hicks.com/lawofattractionsource/index.php

Let's do this together. You and me, it does not matter who is supporting your new life right now. What matters is that you love yourself too much to waste enough precious time to live your purpose in life. Keep this book with you at all times. This book is your companion to emerge into your brand-new you. I am here for you. Remember, the universe adores you, and life is fun. Keep shining your light, my spiritual friend.

I believe in you, and God is waiting to enter your heart like never before. Believe in yourself, and declare your truth to the world. I am powerful! I am magnificent! I am a radiant light that shines everlasting love to the world! Yeah, baby, welcome home!

Namaste.

"Who looks outside, dreams; who looks inside, awakes."

- Carl Gustav Jung

Part Two

Victimhood: Where the Journey Begins

"I have been all things unholy. If God can work through me, he can work through anyone."

- Francis of Assisi

Chapter 4

Overcoming Addictions

Addiction is the state of being enslaved to a habit, practice, or something that is psychologically habit-forming as substance abuse to such an extent that its cessation causes severe trauma. Addiction .(n.d.). In Merriam Webster Dictionary Online, Retrieved August 23, 2014 from <u>http://www.merriam-webster.com/dictionary/addiction</u>.

This chapter is dedicated to get to your core of addictions, whatever they might be, either alcohol, drugs, sex, food, emotional eating, excessive working out, gambling, pornography, personal-growth seminars, relationships, and so forth. These are several forms of addictions we might be experiencing in our life right now. If this resonates like something real for you, great. Let's get to the core of why we are addicted.

Our ego self loves to control our life through addictions. It is that ugly, dark, rejected part of ourselves that we refuse to face head-on. Why? That would make us accountable to get to the core of our sadness and regrets in our lives. Our addictions come from negative self-beliefs that we try our hardest to suppress deep in the attic of our subconscious mind. We do not want to face our past: the mistakes and disappointments about what could have been if only we didn't give up on our dreams. Our negative beliefs about who we are created this destructive mask that takes form of our addiction to control and destroy our lives.

How do we overcome our addictions? The first step is to admit that you have a problem and break the denial about the addiction. Once that's done, now you are ready to conquer the addiction face-to-face with an open heart and mind. In order for that to happen, we must be really tired of abusing our body and spirit. This takes tremendous amount of self-love and God's help to heal and cure you from your addictions. Our physical self can't overcome the dark side of our soul all on its own. It requires the power of God and the universe to restore you back to wholeness and cast out your addictions for good.

How do I know this topic so well? Throughout my life, I went through several addictions trying to cope with my childhood abuse. These addictions were so strong that they were overpowering me. My past was so deeply buried in my soul that the pain was unbearable to deal with while sober, so something had to help me get through the day. At first, from the time I was sixteen years old, exercise became my addiction that helped me deal with the abuse at home. I would work out seven days a week, twice a day, training the same body parts as three hours prior. I remember feeling the high of getting my pump (blood in the muscles) that would help me escape from my pain of my abuse.

My story represents faith in God, hope, forgiveness and love for yourself and others. When we shrink and allow our addictions to control our lives, we are not living to our purest, God-given potential. We must be ready to tell a new story, one with miracles, magic, and possibility.

There comes a time in our life when we must say out loud, "Enough already." Something has to change, and that something is me. I have to change. I had to love myself enough to stop the drama and chaos in my mind.

Your addictions live in your story, period. But what are you prepared to do about it? You see, if you were not aware of your victim story, then I would have some compassion and empathy for you. But when you have done extensive amount of inner work and prayer, meditated, and gone to retreats for healing and transformation, that's when I draw the line in the sand for you and say, "Enough already." My spiritual warrior, it's time to tell a new story of triumph.

Let go of your story, regardless of how horrible and bad it is. Remember this. It's a story you gave life and reality to in your mind. It's time to let that story go and start living your truth. Be who you say you are, and follow through with your plans for this year.

As I became older in my early to late twenties, there couldn't be a day that I missed going to the gym. I felt like a crack addict dying to receive his next high. Even though exercise kept me in great shape, it was addicting; plus, it provided an armor to protect myself from the world. I was extremely strict with my diet and workouts. There was no room for flexibility, and my addictions spilled over to me being in codependent relationships, alcohol, sex, and emotional eating.

Many nights, I would have this intense desire to eat bad food like ice cream, cookies, steak sandwiches, chips, and so forth. These addictions practically ran my life until I finally had enough and asked God for His help. Through the grace and mercy of God, I was cured from my addictions of food, alcohol, and codependent relationships.

Today, January 1, 2014, makes one year of being sober from alcohol. This was possible because I got to the root of my addictions. My sexual abuse was the story that kept me small and from living my full potential. This secret of sexual abuse and molestation was the core of all my addictions. The only way that

I could become free from my past was to share my story with the world and let it go.

I am no longer ashamed of my past. Before, my story kept me in a dark, small coffin I tried to break free from over twenty years. The power of sharing your story is that whatever addictions were attached to story, they die now, period. This chapter will set you free from your past.

Take out a piece of paper, and write down your story. Really get into the emotions and addictions of your past story. As you are writing your story, feel yourself letting go of what no longer serves you. Ask God and His divine guidance to heal you from your addictions and set yourself free.

Next, write down what you are ready to let go. For example:

- I am letting go of my feeling of unworthiness.
- I am letting go of fear of success.
- I am letting go of my victim story for good.
- I am letting go of my scarcity mentality.

Write down anything that no longer serves your highest good. Once you have written down everything from your past, now it is time to rip the paper into bits of pieces. Feel the negative energy dissolving as you set yourself free from your past.

Now on this page, affirm your new story. For example:

- I am a child of God.
- My body is healthy, strong, and lean.
- My soul mate is on his or her way.

Declare and believe that God wants you to prosper in all areas of your life. You are no longer in bondage from your addictions or the past. Affirm all the good you were afraid to ask God for. Omnipresence wants to give you the kingdom of milk and honey.

Abundance and prosperity is our birthright. Declare and affirm your God today. Be grateful and thankful for your life. Rejoice in the resurrection to the brand-new you.

Sing the song of happiness
Sing the song of joy
Sing the song of peace
Sing the song of love
Welcome home, my spiritual seeker

This is the journey to Awaken the Brand-New You. Namaste.

Luis Soto Jr

Affirm your new story with me.

Chapter 5

My Belief in God

As I shared my story with the world about my sexual abuse, the only source that helped me get through my pain, struggle, drama, and addictions was my belief in God. Some people might feel offended or uneasy listening to the word "God." For me, God represents life, energy, freedom, love, universe, divine mind, omnipresence, forgiveness, gratitude, and anything that makes you feel good. He is a power greater than yourself. Whatever name feels comfortable for you to use, then that's how you connect to your source of inspiration.

God's love carried me through my darkness, loneliness, days, and nights. At times, the emotions of my sexual abuse led me to try to kill myself. I vividly recalled one winter night when I was in my apartment alone, depressed and sad that business was slow. I would lie in my bed, hoping to never wake up again from the boredom I felt at that moment in time. Being in that state of mind, you tend to attract more destructive and negative thoughts to your mind.

I heard this voice in my head that told me to just end my sorrow. I got up from my bed, pulled open the kitchen drawer, took a knife, and placed it on my jugular. That was the first and last time I repeated a suicide attempt; I was scared for days afterwards. My faith and belief in God saw me through that lowest point in my life.

All my life, I have always been a believer in God. When I was a teenager, I was fascinated with reading stories about people who have had near-death experiences. I remember praying to God for a near-death experience so I could wake up from this coma I was living my life in. People who had a near-death experience come back to tell of their encounters with this beautiful, shining, bright, loving light that would show them their lives in a panoramic screen in their minds. They see deceased family members and friends walking in this deep, long tunnel and flashes of how they were living their life. The radiant light asks them if they wanted to go back to their lives or stay in this place where love was the energy surrounding them. I always would imagine what that would feel like for me and how that experience would change my life forever.

When I was a child lying in my bed one night, I had an out-of-body experience. My body was lying still in bed, and all of a sudden, my spirit hovered above my body, and I experienced this peace that was so silent that I could have stayed there forever. Looking down at my sleeping body, I was able to escape any chaos that was taking place at home. I slowly descended back to my body and went back to sleep. Just writing about that experience now gives me confirmation that God was always by my side.

My spiritual background comes from New Thought/Metaphysic Christianity. I've been a member of Unity Church of Christ for the past eight years. Here is where I really learned to nurture my understanding and belief in God. In Unity, we believe that there is only one presence and one power in the universe and our life, God, who is all good and omnipotent. Our teaching comes from the life of Jesus the Christ and how to awaken the Christ consciousness in ourselves. We welcome all faiths, and it's a nondenominational organization that promotes "a way of life that leads to health, prosperity, happiness, and peace of mind. Unity helps people deepen their understanding and relationship with God through prayer and meditation."

In order for us to Awaken the Brand-New You, there must be something bigger than ourselves driving our lives. Our human self is limited and cannot expand in consciousness alone. Our spirit is the driving force that awakens all of our spiritual faculties to truly live our truth and serve humanity in a powerful way.

Having belief in God lets you know that something is out there. This source of inspiration truly has your back, no matter what situation you are going through in your life. A belief in God sets the stage for us to transcend our limiting beliefs about who we were in the past to who we are becoming in the present moment. God only wants the best for his children who serve him earnestly. Just thinking about God and wishing for a miracle is not enough for the Almighty Presence to beckon at your call. This sense of oneness and universal love is what so many of world religions and philosophies teach. This is the nectar of your best life.

Now it is time to ask, "What is your belief in God, something greater and more powerful than you?"

Take this next page to write your belief about God and the way this omnipresent source of love has helped you in your life. I believe that we sometimes need to be reminded of all the blessings we have (e.g, the times when there seemed to be no way out and miraculously we came out of the situation better and wiser.) Really think deeply about your belief in God and the way you can improve and deepen your relationship with the omnipotent, powerful source of the universe. Play some relaxing, meditative music to connect your spirit and mind to God. Remember all the exercises in this book are to create awareness of your divine self and Awaken the Brand-New You. Namaste, my spiritual warrior.

Luis Soto Jr

What are your beliefs about God?

* * *

Welcome back, spiritual warrior. How was the exercise for you? Did you gain more awareness about your relationship with God? Are you ready to step up your game with your spiritual practice? I know you are. You wouldn't be reading my book if you weren't ready to progress and unfold to your next level of spiritual maturity. Now it is the time to strengthen your relationship with God. This is your season to live your best self ever.

How do we deepen our belief with God? One of the best ways is prayer and meditation. Prayer is considered speaking to God, and meditation is when we get still and quiet to listen to the still, small voice in the silence. God, the universe, and infinite mind live in the silence. We must be ready to go deep in the silence to experience the answers we are seeking for. I know being silent is difficult, especially when we are subjected to so much noise from the outside world and our internal dialogue. The key here is to have the willingness and yearning to have God closer in your heart. That intention will create the discipline to get quiet and practice being in the silence. Once you commit to a closer relationship with the source of all life, the universe will conspire with your intention by providing you the people, places, and inspiration for divine guidance in your life.

Another way of connecting to God is by journaling. This spiritual tool allows you to express your emotions on paper or in digital format, including your questions or the type of guidance you are seeking to better your life. Journaling is a powerful tool for self-reflection and self-care. You are taking time out of your busy life to connect to your heart and spirit and get more in touch with your divinity. It does not matter if the spelling and grammar are incorrect. What matters most of all is your ability to be vulnerable and open to allow God to come into your life.

When we drop all the layers of our false self (ego) and get naked on paper, that's when we experience the omnipresence in our heart. That's the beginning of dropping your victim story and living your truth.

Another way of experiencing a deeper relationship with God is yoga. Yoga is the bridge that connects your mind, body, and spirit in one session. The practice of yoga allows you to show up on your mat vulnerable, uncertain of what will happen next on your mat and in your life. Connecting to God is exercising all our faculties—mind, body, and spirit—to foster and nurture our divine gifts and talent to the world. The yoga practice opens the channel of your spirit to receive love, guidance, and wisdom from a divine source. The deeper your yoga practice is, the more connected you become to God. Also, yoga offers powerful mantras that illuminate the power centers in your body (chakras) that connect deep to your source of love. The mantras represent life-transforming energy that transcends your ego and opens up your heart and mind to the divine in you. They also help you stay focused on a word or meaning to keep the mind still and undistracted from your monkey chatter mind.

These are some of the strongest ways to deepen your belief with God. Make this the year that you give yourself fully to this omnipotent presence in your life. I know you yearn for God's love. Whoever is reading this book with a history of childhood abuse, I encourage you to trust your gut. Your wisdom never lies. Surrender to the practice of loving God. Release everything that no longer serves your highest good. Love God with all your heart and soul. The more you love God, the more you love yourself. We are all a manifestation of God. The time has come to let go and let God heal your life. I pray for your courage, strength, and willingness to connect to your God, however you relate to it in your consciousness. We are all one in spirit. When one is victorious, we're all winners. This is your season. Welcome, spiritual warrior, to the brand-new you.

Chapter 6

Confronted by My Past

How many times in life are we confronted by our past? When we finally decide to take action and start the process of creating new possibilities in our life, what happens to us? Our past reappears big time to try to stop us in our tracks. Why do you think this happens?

I believe that the intention that we set forth to the universe starts to attract situations, experiences, and circumstances to help us break free from our past. For example, let's say that your New Year's resolution is to lose weight. Instantly, the universe starts to provide opportunities to test your commitment to your goal. It is like your soul is calling forth opportunities to evolve to its next manifestation in this physical life. So the universe conspires, and everyone you know starts to test how badly you want to lose weight and change those negative habits into positive ones to coincide with your weight loss goal.

When I was going through my dark period, feeling sad, isolated, depressed, lonely, and defeated with myself, I attracted exactly what I was putting out into the universe. That is called the law of attraction. We attract exactly what we think and feel about all the time. In essence, that is exactly like asking your past to revisit you every day. When I started therapy for the first time, I remember wanting to run away from my past. Confronted by our past means running away from our hurt.

I went to different seminars, workshops, and retreats, trying my best to run away from my pain that existed in my heart. The past was always there to remind me that, wherever I go, the pain and hurt goes as well. I would go to extreme measures like erasing all my contacts on my phone, changing my phone number that I had had for almost fifteen years, and relocating my residency without telling anyone where I lived, including my family. My thinking on how to leave my past behind, wishing it never took place in my life. My idea was that this would provide a clean slate to start something new. The problem with that idea is that, in order to create newness, there can't be unfinished business in your space.

Think about this. What good does it do when you pretend to be this spiritual person, being positive and smiling and trying your best to cover up all your dirty garbage from the past? This type of living is inauthentic, and eventually, your garbage will seep out from the perfect picture you are trying to portray to the world. Looking back now on all my antics and rituals that kept me locked in my story, I can see clearly how bad luck, scarcity, and unfortunate events kept recycling in my life. I was the attractor of all my drama and chaos in my life. When you are able to admit your mistakes and not hold yourself accountable for all your past actions, then you are free from your past. This awareness happens when we release our secrets that had kept us mute all our lives. There is no power and self-expression of who you really are.

Your past will continue to haunt you if you don't let go of your victim story. Take my story, and allow yourself to break the chains and bondage of denial, shame, and embarrassment for your mistakes and your hurt. God, the omnipotent presence of the universe, is here to set you free from your past. We were all made from His image and likeness; therefore, we also are unlimited to what we can create and be in our lives. The power that exists in God lives to breathe inside of you. The breath is our reminder that we are alive and present in our body. Just breathe into the presence of infinite wisdom and divine mind and allow yourself to receive the gift of redemption in your life. You are no longer a hostage of your story. Let it go, and rejoice in your resurrection today. The world has been waiting for your magnificence, and it's time to share your gifts to the world.

Take this time now, and ask yourself how your past has confronted you, wishing and praying that you were a different person and living someone else's life. I also believe that is why reality TV is so popular in our society today. No one wants to deal with his/ her life and he/ she would rather live vicariously through someone else. This way, there is no expectation or accountability to do something great with our lives.

Here's the good part. This book is about providing you a sacred space to heal, confess, and live a new life. In order for that to take place, we must be willing to fight for our lives and step on our demons from the past. Envision yourself going to war with yourself, not someone else. This battle takes place inside your mind and spirit. The ego wants to keep you small and locked up in your coffin to die. Spirit and omnipresence wants you to live your truth and set yourself free from your past. In order to win, we must be a spiritual warrior and do our inner work so God can heal our hearts, minds, and spirit.

All the exercises in this book are geared to awaken your dormant faculties and create anew. Don't take this lightly, merely reading the chapters one by one and think you will receive the gifts of the spirit. This is your life. Take ownership today, and set yourself free. Let's do this together.

Luis Soto Jr

 Write down on this page what are you running away from this time. We tend to disguise our past by incorporating new people, places, and things to keep us distracted from facing reality and our truth. Remember, this book is your sanctuary where you can be honest, open, and vulnerable where no one is going to judge you. Let the journey begin.

*   *   *

Welcome back, spiritual warrior. What came up for you in this exercise? Maybe you finally allowed yourself to cry and feel your pain. If this is the first time you have been honest with yourself, then the emotions will be pretty strong and confusing at times. That's okay. Embrace the process of letting go, and don't hold back from opening up to yourself. As you continue to read this book, I will provide support, resources, and tools to help and guide you to awaken to the brand-new you.

I decided to share my story about my sexual abuse so we can liberate ourselves together from our past. This is how we take our unique experience and turn it into gold. Once we transform our past, now we have room to create anything we want from a place of love, forgiveness, and gratitude. It's time to stop running away from your past and start running deeper into the brand-new you. This is your season to shine your light and to declare and create a wonderful, spectacular you.

Thank you for your participation with this exercise. I only wish for you freedom, peace of mind, success in all you do, and abundance and love for the brand-new you. You are beautiful, and God loves you. Namaste.

"People only see what they are prepared to see."

- Ralph Waldo Emerson

Part Three

The Light Is Both Near and Far from You

"What we think determines what happens to us, so if we want to change our lives, we need to stretch our minds."

- Dr. Wayne Dyer

Chapter 7

The Road to Recovery

A Buddhist proverb says, "When the student is ready, the teacher will appear." I believe that is true. When we are ready to change our ways, that's when our teacher appears in our lives. It may come to you as a book, friend, or mentor. The universe finds interesting ways to manifest exactly what you need to further your expansion into the brand-new you. So this courageous spiritual warrior decided to seek out the "underground world of recovery" to find refuge from the pain of his sexual abuse. I went to several twelve-step programs out there: AA, SLAA, and NA. They all had their own uniqueness and purpose for their members. As I say, "Everything is manageable, one day at a time."

A twelve-step program is a set of guiding principles (accepted by members as "spiritual principles" based on the approved literature) outlining a course of action for recovery from addiction, compulsion, or other behavioral problems. Originally proposed by Alcoholics Anonymous (AA) as a method of recovery from alcoholism, the twelve steps were first published in *Alcoholics Anonymous: The Story of How More Than One Hundred Men Have Recovered from Alcoholism* in 1939. The method was then adapted and became the foundation of other twelve-step programs. As the American Psychological Association summarizes, the process involves the following: *W.,B. (n.d.). Alcoholics Anonymous. Retrieved from http:/www.aa.org/pages/en_US*

- Admitting that one cannot control one's addiction or compulsion;
- Recognizing a higher power that can give strength;
- Examining past errors with the help of a sponsor (experienced member);
- Making amends for these errors;
- Learning to live a new life with a new code of behavior;
- Helping others who suffer from the same addictions or compulsions

One of the most effective ways of working on the program is having an experienced sponsor walk you through the steps. This program for recovery takes patience, courage, and a willingness to change your old way of being. I was introduced to the twelve steps when I was working with a therapist who specializes with men who had been sexually abused. He suggested I go to a meeting and see how I felt about it. At first, I felt embarrassment about going to a support group for my problem. But I really needed support, and like my therapist told me, one main thing I had in common with everyone in the group was that I couldn't be okay with myself. I did not accept myself for who I was. The sexual abuse story had (already taken over my mind // kept me hostage.

I started going to meetings and became better acquainted with the groups. I belonged to several groups, and my life was about attending meetings, working the steps with my sponsor, working out, and keeping to myself. My family and friends did not know where I was living or what I was doing with my life. I still managed to work and train my clients to pay for my necessity for living. My clients would ask me what was wrong. They could sense a deep sadness inside of me. I wouldn't even try to dress nicely or fix myself up. I was in recovery, and that was how I felt every day.

The awareness I have about this now is that it didn't have to be extreme, but my vulnerable emotions were falsely misleading me to believe that something was wrong with me. In a way, I was abusing myself with my past and repeating memories that brought up pain, hurt, and resentment in my soul. I remember waking up in the middle of the night, wondering, "How did I get here?" I was confused, lost, ashamed, and embarrassed with myself. I would ask God why I was going through this darkness. I could not accept that I was going to be in recovery all my life. Nor was I going to admit to myself that I would always be an addict and there was nothing I could do about it.

This is my opinion about the twelve steps of recovery. I feel that the steps do provide a roadmap to recovery, but it is not complete. My belief is that our soul is here to expand and evolve into who we are born to be. Therefore, recovery is only a part of that equation. If there is a problem or addiction that needs our attention, recovery is the answer from when we recover and heal from our past. Then we must be ready to go into our next stage of development. I will go deeper into what I'm referring to in the following chapters, which will piece together the whole story nicely.

But for now, think about this for a moment. If we stay in recovery all our lives, then how can we create and expand in our creativity and zest for life? Once we go through the necessary steps in our process of getting better, then it is time for something new and different to create and establish new beliefs about who you are. God did not make a mistake with us. We are all born with the divinity and power of the Most High.

The question really becomes, "How badly do we want to change our lives?" If one addiction is under control, then why do we ignore the other ones that are taking the old ones' place? That's not recovering from an addiction. That is substituting one for the other. I'm not bringing this up because I want to fight and discount the changes that the groups have done for thousands of people all over the world. My view is that the twelve steps group was founded over seventy-six years ago.

This is a new era of possibility for the world at large. It is time to try new approaches to awakening to the brand-new you. Addictions will take over our lives if we continue to tell the old story of our past. It's time to believe in your heart and mind that the power and grace of the divine heals you. If you keep the idea that you will be always an addict, then we are making room in our consciousness for that to happen to us. Instead, believe that you have gone through the recovery stage and now you are ready to live boldly, powerfully, and alive.

I remember people would try to convince me that this was who I was, "I'm an addict, and there is nothing I can do about it." I couldn't accept that statement or faith in my soul. I knew God, the omnipotent presence, made me more than an addict. I was a victim of my sexual abuse story but not an addict. I was addicted to my past like an addict is addicted to his or her drug of choice. Once I was ready to release my sad victim story, then my mind started to see new possibilities in my horizon. I moved out from the apartment that was kept secret from everyone in my life. I relocated back to the city, filled with this palpable energy of excitement, enthusiasm, and passion to live your dreams. I focused on building my business up again and left that chapter of recovery in my past.

Now that I'm writing this book, I am starting to connect the dots of my experiences. I realized why I had to experience and endure those difficult and challenging moments in my life. I had no idea that I would be writing a book about my Awakening to the Brand-New You. I would think about it like a fantasy that was not possible for me.

I knew I had a lot to share with the world, but my faith in myself was not as big as God's faith in me. Even when I moved back to the city and started to live a clean, sober life from addiction, I was successful for a year, and then my childhood abuse pain continued to surface again in my life. I decided that I would create my own recovery program to live a sober life and have fun without my addictions. I started thinking of ways that I could stay clean and have fun at the same time. I decided to start taking salsa classes to meet new people, learn how to dance, and live a sober life.

In the beginning, I was having a great time, going to social parties with my dance group, staying sober, and dating people for fun times. The summertime was the most challenging time for me to stay clean from drinking. When I would go on dates, the women would find it weird I didn't drink, and eventually, I succumbed to my addiction. Again, I tried to sustain another intimate relationship with someone, and I couldn't do it. My drinking became a daily habit to keep me happy and keep my friends around. I knew it was time to go back to therapy, but this time, I was looking for a spiritual mentor to help me with the issue of my past. The universe provided this therapist who was affordable and really grounded me in what I was looking for in my life.

He was the person who brought to my awareness how shame and guilt were running my life. Prior to this, I had no idea how these two enemies were governing my life. We decided to create a program for me to stay connected to people, not drink, and heal from my past. He would always remind me that, if we didn't talk about what happened with my brother in detail, then we were not really working the therapy. My problem was that I could not be alone any period of time. I would be involved in codependent relationships with women simply because I wanted the company and nothing else. That is not a good enough reason to be with someone, but I was desperate and scared in facing my demons alone so the company would help me stay grounded for a while.

One of the ways for me to stay grounded in my therapy was to belong to a meditation group. This would help me connect with people on a spiritual level, along with making new friends… staying sober from drinking. I started taking classes in Buddhism to deepen my spiritual practice and learn how to be independent. The classes I took were beneficial, and they help me stay on my path toward living a new life. Again, I want to stress that, when we are working to the core of our problem, the addictions will come after you with vengeance. Remember, that is part of the process of Awakening to the Brand-New You. When that happens, don't fight the process. You may or may not be strong enough to overcome the urge to fall prey to the addictions or not. The main thing here is to never give up on yourself, no matter what life throws at you. You are stronger than your addictions and your victim stories of abuse, shame, and regret. Always remember that the universe wants you to win and prevail in your life. Nothing is too difficult to overcome as long as your belief in God is solid.

This is our journey to live our truth in the world. There comes a time when we have to play big in order to really make drastic changes in our life. Don't stay content with what you have and who you are. There is more to discover about the amazing human being you are. Reading this book is a sign from the universe to let you know that there is more for you to learn, grow, and expand the awareness of your powerful self.

Take this sign, and hold it close to your heart. We are all here to share the majesty of who we are. Believe this truth, and set yourself free for good. Examine your life right now, and ask yourself, "What is not working?" Be brutally honest with yourself, and take this time for self-reflection back to your soul. Your spirit knows what is right for you. Look for the feeling in your body, and see how your intuition speaks to you. Deep down in our gut, we know what needs to change in order for us to live our purpose.

I always knew that I would be speaking all over the world about transformation and spirituality, but I was afraid of letting my story die. That victim story has kept me locked up for over twenty years of my life.

How long has your story from the past kept you in bondage of unraveling yourself? Please do not beat yourself up about how much time has been lost. This is about having enough courage now to break free from your past. Just like a butterfly that represents transformation, spread your wings, and fly high into the sky of your new life.

Take this next page, and get clear on what no longer serves your highest good. Be ready to eradicate all the negative thinking out of your life and consciousness. The more clarity you have with this exercise, the more powerful the transformation will be for you. I am here as your Transformational Life Coach leading you to the brand-new you. Take flight, warrior. This is your new life.

Luis Soto Jr

    Write down what no longer serves your highest good.

* * *

Awesome work, spiritual warrior. Now it is time to make a declaration to yourself and the universe.

> I _____ declare that I am no longer tolerating mediocrity in my life. This old chapter no longer exists in my mind and consciousness. I am free from this person, place, or experience that lives only in my past. Today _____ (date), I set myself free for good and open my arms to receiving only good in my life. I affirm that this statement is true, and I give my word of honor that I will not be a victim ever again. Through the power of the omnipresence, God, universal mind, and infinite wisdom, this is established as law, and so it is.
>
> Name _____
> Date _____

Congratulations on taking the first steps toward changing your life. I commend you for your courage and integrity to love yourself enough to stop the drama and chaos in your life. You are now free to be yourself. Namaste.

Chapter 8

The Will to Persevere

All throughout my adulthood, I struggled with the word "perseverance." I felt that I was not making enough progress. But in reality, I did. I could remember starting a project or trying to finish a certification course that I just didn't want to complete. I lacked intention pushing me to reach my goals. All my credentials were collecting dust on the floor, and I was not aware of all my accomplishments until I had an awakening from within one day. Out from the silence, a still, small voice whispered in my ear, "It's time to live your purpose in life." From that moment on, my bad behavior and habits shifted from being lazy and not focused to urgency. Life began to matter because I mattered.

To persevere means to be determined and not stop until you achieve your goal. It is about being tenacious and fixated on what is important for you to manifest in your life. Writing this book is a great example of persevering. As I write this chapter, I can feel the urgency and enthusiasm branching out to all who will read my book. Maybe right now, you are at a crossroad in your project or goal, and something inside of you wants to quit. You feel like, "Why bother? No one really cares if I finish or not."

Here's the secret. The world cares, I care, and God cares. What you have inside you is unique and special to the world. Your contribution is paramount, and please don't ever forget it. Our fears are indicators that lead us to do our greatest work if we allow ourselves to go on the journey to self-exploration and transformation. Think about how long you have been putting this off from your to-do list. Each day becomes the same as the following day. Instead of working toward your goal, you deviate and do something that is not related to your goal. You organize your closet, pay bills, watch TV, eat food, have a drink, go to a movie, and escape from your fear of playing big and winning your game in life.

Right this second, I'm entrenched in the deepest gratitude while writing this book. I strongly feel that the essence and presence of the omnipotent source of all good, God, is writing through me now. Spirit has a divine way of manifesting itself on paper when you allow yourself to be the conduit to share this power message to the world. I can see my book being published, transforming the reader to persevere and live his/ her best life ever. The joy in my heart is enormous, and I thank God for using me as his vessel to share this divine message to all the spiritual seekers out there. This is your moment to shine, persevere, and complete what you have started.

Many times in my life, I would start something with great excitement and enthusiasm, but I would give up the moment I reached my comfort zone threshold. Why? I was so conditioned at a very young age to not try anything new because I felt I didn't have the intelligence to carry it out in my life. Our upbringing has a lot to do with how we conduct and maneuver ourselves in our daily lives. The good news is that you have a choice to stop that negative pattern and replace that negative thought for this new belief. I can, I'm able, and I'm capable of accomplishing anything I put my mind to with the guidance and power of God. We are all fabulous, and our talents and gifts have been buried deep within us for too long now. Remember, powerful spiritual warrior, this is your season to shine your light and claim your inheritance to the kingdom of God. Abundance and prosperity is your birthright. Rejoice and say, "Hallelujah!"

Let's really play deep in this field of unlimited possibilities. The way to receive your transformation and benefit from reading this book is by doing the exercises. These exercises are here to create awareness with yourself and your goals in life. They will provide tremendous insight, structure, and support to break through any hidden inner blocks that are lurking deep in your subconscious mind. Make yourself proud, and participate full throttle with this book. I am here to guide and nurture you to Awaken the Brand-New You.

Write down three things that have been on the back burner for some time now. Really think about what life would be like if these three things were completed. Remember, we are doing this together, so let the games begin.

1.

2.

3.

Once you have written the list, pick one that really needs to be done ASAP. For me, it's the completion of this book. The faster I complete the book, the faster people will benefit from my work, and transformation will take over the world. No matter what has been holding you back from the past, take action today, and continue from where you left off.

No time has been wasted. It's only time gained because you have a new awareness in consciousness. This is your moment to prove to yourself that you have what it takes to live big and win. Take the rest of this page to complete the exercise, and we'll connect soon. Attack with perseverance and power for God. Go for it.

* * *

Welcome back, spiritual warrior. I want to commend you on really diving deep in the process of Awakening the Brand-New You. You are doing a fantastic job, and I'm very proud of you.

The interesting thing about persevering is that, once you start, you pick up momentum to continue to your next goal. There is tremendous power in following through to the end, regardless of how long it takes to complete the task at hand. You develop character, trust in yourself and others, and the ability to complete anything that comes your way. This will help you in breaking old beliefs that you thought were facts.

Here's the interesting thing about that. If you truly believe that you are dumb, then the mind will act according to your belief. Remember, someone believing that he/she is dumb or not good enough is a false belief, not a fact. A fact is $2 + 2 = 4$. A fact is not that you are dumb or unworthy. That's a belief, and the beauty about that is that we can change the new belief to empower us versus disempower us. A belief is something you constituted in your mind that seems to appear real, but in reality, it's not.

With this newfound knowledge, you can test your new beliefs to take on bigger challenges in life. Let's repeat these powerful affirmations to make this new belief concrete in our subconscious mind:

- "I am smart."
- "I am powerful."
- "I am love."
- "I am enough."
- "I am that I am."

Recite these powerful affirmations to yourself morning or night. Allow the power of spirit to transcend your negative belief about yourself to a beautiful, powerful belief of certainty. You are blessed, and God loves you. Namaste.

Chapter 9

Putting All the Pieces Together

As I look back into my childhood and remember all the abuse I endured—the trauma to my body, my spirit torn apart, and no sense of direction in life—finally after twenty years of diligent, steadfast commitment to not giving up and moving forward, even though my life felt like it was upside down, I am finally at peace with myself and my past. I believe life will give you what you do and don't deserve. What I am referring to here is that every event, episode, circumstance, and person that has taken place in our lives is part of the puzzle. Putting all the pieces together really means connecting the dots from where you started and where you are today. Back then, I had no idea that I would be writing a book and sharing it with the world. I always knew that I wanted to make an impactful difference in the world, but my past would always bring me down to my knees in sorrow, regret, guilt, and shame. The truth is that our life was made to order before we were born. I believe we get to choose our path to fulfill our prophecy inside of us. Our greatest gift comes from truly taking all the raw materials from our past and transforming it into the brand-new you.

For a long time in my life, I would push my past away from me and run as fast as I could, wishing for more new materials to play with. I condemned my past. The past was too hurtful for me to embrace. I wish things were different and I was a different person all together. I rejected myself, and there was no love for me. It is really amazing now to see clearly how all the pieces have come together in divine order, and I am at peace with me. There comes a time in our life when the lights come on inside our minds and consciousness. We can see that everything makes perfect sense now. Before in the past, I kept on asking God, "When is all this suffering and all the lessons learned going to pay off in my life?"

I would wait for a response, a divine sign that my message was being received, but I would just say to myself, "Everything is always in divine order." That affirmation would give me the security and sign I needed to stay grounded in spirit.

What does it really mean to put all the pieces together? For me, it is about looking back at your life from this vantage point and observing the journey through the eyes of love, forgiveness, and gratitude for all the experiences and spiritual exams we had to pass in order to be free from our pasts. You see, our past was divinely orchestrated even before we were born. The life purpose, our dharma, we eagerly seek to find lives in our past.

Please understand that, if you experienced something horrific like sexual abuse, rape, or any type of injustice done to you, then my heart goes out to you. I can sincerely empathize with your pain. For a long time, I rejected the realization that I was a victim of sexual abuse. The denial and cover-up for my hurt resulted in all types of addictions like alcohol, food, sex, and relationships. That was my way of trying to forget my past.

I truly had no idea how, forty-six years later, I would see the beauty in the tapestry of my life so clearly now.

I no longer hide from my pain or my past. That defining experience has led me to writing my book and sharing my story about love, forgiveness, and gratitude to the world. Who I am this moment is an author, speaker, and life coach; my past made me the man I am today. Before, what was darkness in my past was the creation and molding of my character. There is no more hurt in my life. The past represents an experience in time that gave me clarity, strength, hope, determination, and resilience to help people heal themselves through self-reflection, personal development, and spirituality.

My intention for anyone who has had traumatic experiences in their upbringing is to understand that the moment has come to leave their past behind and shine his/her light of truth to the world. No more hiding or running away from your past. You are free. I know you must be thinking that I'm crazy and, "How dare you pretend like nothing happened to me?" On the contrary, I know your suffering and pain, but it's time to choose how to view your life from beginning to end.

Whatever situation you're in today, know and understand that it is not a life sentence for you to accept as your destiny. This is an opportunity to put the pieces together and witness all the synchronicity, missed moments, and valuable lessons that the universe presented to you so you could learn your calling in life. The universe gives us a compass with a manual inside of our being so we can tap into our greatness.

I thought that the lessons could be learned by hearing about them through other people, but the mystery, the secret that is our life, is a masterpiece of our past. Try to stay with me right now. If you can understand what I'm explaining, then you will experience a massive quantum leap in the trajectory of your life. Until now, you might have been held in bondage and enslaved by your past. Who you are today resembles the pain, misfortune, and drama that the past brought to you.

Okay, let's say that it is not true. Please hear me out before you stop reading the book. You already know that this is not the life you want to live right now. So let's look at all the pieces in your past and see clearly why we had to endure such hardship in order to live our calling in life.

For example, let's say that you grew up in an environment infested with drugs, alcohol, and violence. Because of your upbringing, you got involved with drugs and alcohol at a young age, which led to covering up the pain inside of you. Fast-forward to today. You are now addicted to alcohol and drugs and have tried many times to rehabilitate yourself from this addiction, but deep down inside, something tells you, "Don't give up." That voice inside of you is your dharma in life. If you can see all the pieces in your life through the eyes of love, forgiveness, and gratitude, that will open the gates to your authentic self. The pieces coming together indicate that it is time to live your calling in life and forget about your past.

Take all the pain inside of you, and let it go because it no longer serves your highest good. This is your moment to shine and begin to accept your life just the way it is. This will give you closure and open the reservoir of peace inside your soul.

Today, you will begin the process of loving yourself. The past has served its purpose in your life. Rejoice your divine self. You were made with pure love. The doors are open now for you to live the life you were born to live. Go get it. Live your best life ever.

"Accept everything about yourself—I mean everything, you are you and that is the beginning and the end—no apologies, no regrets."

- Clark Moustakas

Part Four

Embracing Solitude

"We may encounter many defeats but we must not be defeated."

-Maya Angelou

Chapter 10

The Gift of Starting All Over Again

This chapter speaks boldly about the gift of starting all over again in your life. How many times do we make promises to ourselves, family, and friends, but never follow through with our word? I know for myself that, in my journey to Awakening the Brand-New You, I fell numerous times on my face, not caring what other people would think about me.

What truly matters was that I was willing to start all over again from scratch and create new possibilities for my life. Sometimes we may feel embarrassed or upset about messing up big time. That's a normal response on feeling inadequate and not valuing yourself to get the job done. I felt like that most of my life. Through all the accomplishments and inner work I did on myself, it was never enough to satisfy the void that lived in my heart. I managed some way or another to find a way to destroy anything great that was taking place in my life. There was no confidence in my ability to do anything right. Other people would remind me of my talents and gifts, but it didn't matter because I rejected the compliments in the same way that I rejected myself.

When I was involved in the twelve steps program and life felt as though I was not moving forward toward my goal, I would oftentimes say, "It's okay, Luis. We are going to start all over again, and today I did." Think about this. How many times do we keep on repeating negative behaviors because we feel life is not worth doing over? How many times have you fallen short from your diet and decided that it's too late to start all over again? That's the gift we have as human beings that, when we fall on our faces, we have the choice of getting up and starting all over again.

It's never too late to start from a clean slate. Most of the time, we continue on the wrong path because we don't give ourselves permission to do better next time. This type of awareness creates breakthrough and new possibilities. The key is to forgive oneself for not getting it right the first time. Don't continue to torture yourself until you become addicted or, worse yet, can't stop this negative habit that will destroy what you want to give birth to. For myself, starting all over again created new space to explore new thoughts and actions that were not present in my past mistakes and judgment with myself. When I was having financial struggles and living with my parents because I couldn't afford rent on my own, I never lost faith in God or myself, and I would envision one day living in NYC again in my new apartment, proud, happy, and joyous of my accomplishment.

Sometimes we tend to forget how resilient we really are when faced with hard times. I believe that we all have the strength and willpower to overcome any obstacle that is in our way toward greatness. We were born with God-given talents, gifts, and powers that are ready to be awakened within ourselves. But are you ready to go deep to the depth of your being and release that awesomeness that resides in you? I know you have what it takes to wake up the dormant forces at your command. The light that lives in you, lives in God. The omnipresent power of God resides in you.

Take this time now, and think about an experience when you felt there was no way out from this negative situation and you miraculously overcame it. What did you do? How did you overcome this negative obstacle in your life?

Take this next page, and write down how you rose to the occasion and were triumphant. Once you complete this powerful exercise of awareness, I know you will be ready to look at your current situation through new eyes of hope, faith, and love. May the spirit of God guide you toward your past experience and provide insights, revelations, and aha moments that will create new space in your consciousness to start all over again. Start writing.

The journey continues…

*   *   *

I hope you took that exercise seriously and allowed spirit to guide you to awaken your faculties to create anew. You see, these exercises are how you really get to move yourself to another level of awareness that will break through any resistance you may be experiencing right now. If we are not willing to explore our emotions, there is no room for growth in our life. Starting all over again gives you another chance to do better next time.

None of us is perfect. We are all trying to do the best we can with what we have. Don't wish for fewer problems. Wish for more awareness of self. Really go deep inside yourself and surrender to the majesty that you are. Start today to really love and respect yourself and honor your path toward mastery. You are awesome, beautiful, powerful, smart, resilient, and creative.

Today, make a declaration to start honoring your word like it's gold. Our words have the ability to transform our lives and the people around us. There is powerful energy that comes from your throat when you open your mouth and declare your word to the world. The problem is that we have taken our gift to create and start all over again for granted. Right now, you are reading my book that took me to places in my subconscious mind that I didn't know it existed.

I went through resistance, denial, punishment, and torture on not wanting to finish the book. Once I turned that corner and made myself accountable to completing the book, there was no way out for me. The ironic thing is that I love to write, speak, and talk about transformation and spirituality. The universe has already provided the roadmap and completion of my book. That was only possible when I started to leverage the energy and feeling in my body of fear. Once I became aware of why I was avoiding writing the book, then space opened up for me, and I experienced freedom to live in the present moment. This will happen to you if you follow my blueprint to Awakening the Brand-New You.

So why did I procrastinate and waste precious time every day on not completing my book? I believe that, once we have moved past our comfort zone, resistance will resurface in your space. The resistance is really there to move you forward and not backward. That's when you must buckle down, get grounded in spirit, and step into your next phase of spiritual unfoldment. We all have this inner reservoir of tenacity inside of us. In order to tap into this profound sacred space of peace, energy, and light, we have to be out of our comfort zone.

Picture this. Imagine there is a closed door in front of you. Locks, bolts, chains, and cobwebs that have been there for quite some time cover the door. You come face-to-face, staring at this mammoth of a door, asking yourself, "How can I open the door?" Here is the gift of this analogy. The question allows you to see the door as it is. Remember, you imagine the door with locks, bolts, and chains in your mind. Now you can imagine the door without any locks, bolts, and chains because it all exists in your imagination.

The question has allowed you to set yourself free from your past. Use this powerful faculty in your mind. Imagination allows you to see your life unfold in positive or negative physical life. Here is where we create with spirit what is yearning to manifest in our world. Imagine this mammoth door opening now and allowing you to step into your destiny.

That's what starting all over again provides us all. We are on this quest to be the best we can be. No one wants to go through emotional hell if he/she can avoid it. Now is the time to open the door to your next chapter in your life. You have traveled this far to read my book, so now it is time to take action and start all over again.

We are now in a new year of awakening the powers of faith, strength, wisdom, love, power, imagination, understanding, will, renunciation, zeal, divine order, and regeneration. These faculties are part of your spiritual self. This is the year that you stop running away from your fears and live your truth. I know you can do it. I believe in you. This book is your guide to lead you to your magnificence.

Thank you for taking this journey with me. It's time to shine your light. The world is waiting for you. Open your heart, smile, breathe, and be in gratitude. You are now on your way to Awakening the Brand-New You. Namaste.

Chapter 11

The Five Stages of Awakening

What does it mean to be awakened? Is that the same thing as being enlightened? How does someone awaken to his or her authentic self? Is there any hope for me? The process of awakening happens in five stages: Victimhood, Healing, Transformation, Reinventing oneself, and Celebration.

Allow me to explain. Through my observation and diligent search to heal myself from my childhood abuse wounds, I attended numerous life-changing seminars and workshops, twelve-step support programs, therapy, yoga, meditation, and prayer and coaching methodologies that all contributed to creating this blueprint to make you aware of what stage you are in so you can move through the stages with ease and grace. I believe that, in order for us to awaken to the brand-new you, we must be willing to explore new possibilities and allow ourselves to be vulnerable, open, and receptive to this new way of awakening oneself.

Stage 1: Victimhood

We all have to start somewhere on this odyssey journey to self-realization, and victimhood is the most appropriate place to begin. This stage is where our past dictates, governs, and commands our existence in all our actions. There is no freedom to think clearly or be at peace with yourself. This stage is where you really have not accepted your past. You are still in denial about the traumatic events, and you relive them, day in and out. There is a great deal of hurt feeling, along with regret, anger, shame, blame, sadness, and isolation from the world. You live life as a victim of your circumstances, and no one can convince you otherwise. We blame the world for what happened to us, and there is no accountability or responsibility from us. This space feels like life handed us a life sentence.

As you can see, this type of mind-set is operating at a low frequency energy plane. Our family and friends are concerned about our well-being. They fear that we will physically hurt ourselves or get in trouble with the law or people in general. If this place sounds familiar to you, then I encourage you to wake up and smell the roses. Give yourself permission to use judgment-free awareness and be present to this dark, lonely place you are in your mind. There is no freedom to choose, be, or create new reality for yourself. This stage is very critical to acknowledge and accept before we are able to move to the other stages of awakening.

The key word here is "acceptance." If we can't accept this stage with vulnerability and an open heart, then there's no room for our life to change at all. We must feel comfortable, accept our past, and not wish things were different for us. There is a great deal of liberation when we stop running away from our past and accept our story as it is. Here is when things starts to change inside of you, and now you are open to receiving divine guidance to further your spiritual growth.

As we move through each stage, I have a declaration that you will agree to sign to solidify this powerful document of change and awareness of self.

I _____ am a victim, and I accept this stage in my life today. I will no longer be in denial about my past or wish my life were different than it is now. I accept this stage with an open heart and mind and surrender to the process of awakening oneself.

Date _____
Signed _____

Thank you for trusting yourself and your divine guidance within. I commend you on your courage and love for yourself to take this bold step into your new life. Allow yourself to start seeing your life through the eyes of love, forgiveness, and gratitude to help you along the stages of awakening to the Brand-New You. Congratulations on moving to the next stage of awakening.

Remember, there is no rush to move through these stages quickly. Take your time, and honor where you are right now. This is a blueprint to inform you about where you are and what's required to move through the stages with less trouble and more ease. Welcome to stage two.

Stage 2: Healing

This stage is where we have accepted our life 100 percent. We are now ready to heal our heart and wounds from our past, practice forgiveness, and forgive whatever happened to us consciously or unconsciously. Forgiveness is our key to tap into the power of healing.

In this place, you will experience more light, pain, tears, internal earthquakes, sadness, aloneness, desperation, impatience, and solitude. Solitude is being able to be present with yourself and the silence. Embrace all the suppressed emotions that rise to the surface of your conscious mind to set yourself free from the past. Healing can take a couple years to cleanse your body and mind from the past. Everyone's past experience is unique and different. That's why we must start to listen to our intuition to guide us appropriately to our light. I can honestly say that you can stay in victimhood and healing all your life without truly having access to your divine essence and purpose in life.

I know for myself that I would try to pass the stages and avoid the pain that lived in the darkness of my subconscious mind. I wanted to be transformed and move on with my life. The sad part is that I did not have the awareness I'm sharing with you right now. Even though I would make great progress with my life, I needed to stay longer in healing and not rush the process to awaken to the brand-new you.

This is a critical moment for you to decide today if you need more time to heal and forgive or if you decide it's time to leave this stage and embrace your next stage of spiritual unfoldment. Whatever you decide, know that these stages are here to give you guidance and light to move ahead to your new life. I honor your commitment to better yourself and set yourself free from the past. You are a spiritual warrior in my eyes, and God will see you through to the very end. Namaste.

Congratulations, spiritual seeker. You have now made it to stage three.

Stage 3: Transformation

Transformation is an act, process, or instance of transforming or being transformed. It is a change in form, appearance, nature, or character. Stage three is very powerful. In this stage is where you have done enough healing, and now you are ready to transform your mind, body, and spirit.

This place is about exercising our faculties to tap into who we are, our essence. In this space, you will start take seminars and workshops with experimental processes to let go of any dead weight, emotions, and beliefs that no longer serve your highest good. Here, you learn to get still and listen to the still, small voice of truth and liberation. Your intuition is heightened, and your awareness starts to expand in every direction. You start experiencing a metamorphosis of change and transformation from the inside out. Possibilities, freedom, and excitement fill this space, and you want to change every aspect of you. The danger comes when we want to fix ourselves and do over all the events that have transpired in our past.

It is very addicting to stay in this stage because is challenging, fun, scary, and rewarding. I remember going to numerous self-help seminars and hoping to get rid of me and start with a new identity because I rejected every part of me. I even went to the extreme to use a different name and persona because I felt I was better than everyone attending the seminar was. You see, when you are broken deep inside your being, you try to disguise the hurt with arrogance and intimidation, which, in reality, you are a scared little child buried in an adult body pretending that you have your life in order.

I was deeply afraid to leave this stage because it meant I had to stretch far beyond my comfort zone and completely release all the baggage from my past that was still interfering with my new life. It was challenging and nerve-wracking, but I did it so you can have the blueprint to awaken to the brand-new you.

So divine reader, I want you to ask yourself, "How long am I planning to be in this stage?" Think about it. If you have gone to numerous life-changing seminars, workshops, and therapy and you still are afraid to change your life big time, then it is time to let go of your fears and step into your next stage of spiritual development for mind, body, and soul. Now, if you just started going to seminars, workshops, retreats, and therapy, then you are exactly where you need to be.

For the other spiritual warrior, I call forth your courage and willingness to trust your God, the divine presence that is always with you. He/she is the omnipotent spirit of life, love, and universal mind. It's time to release your crutch and step into your greatness.

Congratulations. Welcome to stage four.

Stage 4: Reinventing Oneself

Stage four means to invent again or anew, especially without knowing that the invention already exists inside of you. This stage is life-changing. Here is where, until now, who you were being and living as starts to disappear into your best self. The essence of your being begins to take over your life. Your physical self starts to transform, and you start exercising more, wearing nicer clothes, eating healthier foods, resting more, and being more in touch with your divine nature of God. Life opens the channel for you to access the power of the universe because you feel the oneness and connection of your soul. Your spiritual growth explodes into more contemplated disciplines like yoga, meditation, and Tai Chi.

There is light coming from you and your declaration to serve the universe by living your truth. You are congruent with your beliefs and values. Your purpose, the prophecy of why you were born, starts to manifest in all areas of your life. Your career starts to align your intention of service and contribution to the world. A quantum shift in your thinking starts to break down old negative beliefs, patterns, emotions, and habits that are not in alignment with who you are now.

This stage is where you finally get to do the work you were born to do in this lifetime. This stage is where your past no longer has control of your life. You have made amends with your past, people, and experiences that no longer dominate your conscious God mind. Now you have dominion and mastery over your life.

Here we are, spiritual warrior. Now ask yourself some questions. Am I ready to reinvent myself? What does that look like for me? What is required for me to reinvent myself? If you are asking these questions aloud or silently, then you are ready to reinvent yourself. Congratulations. I knew you could do it. For anyone who is not here yet, please don't be discouraged and upset that someone else is competing with you in your life. The truth is that there is no race and we all arrive in God's time. When we realize that our purpose is to be guided by our intuition and listen to the music inside of us that wants to sing and dance, that's when we arrive home. Wherever you are in this journey to Awakening the Brand-New You, allow yourself to be guided by spirit, accept where you are, and embrace that stage with all your heart and soul.

Before I arrived at this stage, my junk from the past had to be erased. In other words, the events from my past that would keep me hostage in my own mind transcended into blessings and lessons to learn and grow from. This book would not have been written if I were still stuck in the other stages of awakening. I now understand the process and fluidity that it brings to your life. Wherever you are now in this journey, I bow my head down to you and commend your bravery for never giving up and believing in you. Namaste.

Here we are, spiritual warriors. You have made it to stage five.

Stage 5: Celebration

Celebration is the act of celebrating who you are. I am very excited by this stage. When we decide to live our life by what we feel is in alignment with our higher self, then we are truly celebrating life. Most of the time, we are concerned about how people will judge us, trying to look good and feeling inadequate with areas we have not mastered yet in our life. Here is the big truth behind all that nonsense of looking good. "Who cares what people think of you?" This is your life, and you are responsible for your creation.

Celebration is about living your true essence all the time. No more secrets. Embrace your truth, and be authentic with yourself. Release all the negative energy from the past mistakes, people, and experiences, and be at peace. We are all eternal beings who are on this planet for one reason, the expansion of who we are, not someone else's idea or opinion of what is right and wrong for our lives. Be honest and at peace with yourself, and celebrate your light with the world. I believe we sometimes have a challenging time to celebrate our accomplishments and victories because we don't want to brag about ourselves. We'd rather judge and not be gentle with our divine self than acknowledge the greatness and hard work that led us to the winner's circle of life. I believe that society is losing sight of what is true. Making fun of people on videos and exploiting them to show their imperfections is not cool. Bullying innocent children and teens to hide your own insecurities is not funny.

Here's one reason why people want to judge your life. It takes away responsibility and attention from them to live their truth. In life, we all make mistakes that haunt us in our past. We have our ability to make better choices because we have our judgment about ourselves. We let small, insignificant events and people dictate how we should live our lives because of fear of not looking good.

The truth is that, once we stop caring about what others think about us, then and only then can we live our lives in accordance with source energy. We were all created unique and beautiful with our own purpose, a calling in life. How can we live our calling if we are so concerned about what others think about us? We can't. It is impossible to live joyously if we are always covering up our true essence of who we are. Whether you failed a test, got a divorce, lost your job, or hurt yourself physically again and again, so what? It does not matter how many times we failed. What matters is that you keep on trying until you get it right and it is in alignment with your true essence of your soul.

Go ahead and live your life. You don't need permission from anyone. The only one who matters is God and you. Feel deep in your core about who you are and what events and lessons have led you to read this book. There are no coincidences in life, only synchronicity events that happen when we are in alignment with source energy, God.

It is time to set yourself free from your past. Don't look back anymore. There is nothing worth looking back for. Believe in yourself and the majesty of this moment. The universe wants you to live your life, sing your song, dance your dance, and be true to you.

Whatever you have been embarrassed about in the past, this is the defining moment you have been waiting for all your life. No more pretending to be someone you are not. Live your life the way God has intended for you to live. There are no mistakes. There are only valuable lessons that lead us to our higher God self. Rejoice in the magnificence of who you are and who you are becoming. This is spirit affirming your concern today. Live your truth. Be who you are born to be. Your greatest gifts live inside of you. This is the moment to shine your divine light to the world. Live your life. Celebrate your essence and be happy. The power lives inside of you. All the answers are waiting for you deep in the silence of your being. Become silent, and listen to the still, small voice of your magnificence. The universe is waiting for your command to summons the vibration of your truth, the essence of who you are. You are source energy, a powerful, amazingly beautiful being of light. It is time to share your beauty, love, and power with the world.

Declare, spiritual warrior.

Today, I no longer live for other people's approval of me. I am an extension of God, and I call forth my truth to set me free. This is who I am. I am the light. I am beautiful. I am smart. I am a genius. I am talented. I am love. I am that I am.

Signed _____

Date _____

    Our greatest teachers are the experiences that shape and mold our lives. Once we forgive ourselves completely for any harm done unto us, then we will no longer carry the poison in our soul. My intention for writing this book is to create a space for reconciliation with family and friends.

    Think about this for a moment. What good does it bring to anyone who is still holding a grudge about what happened in the past? Nothing. Stop and press pause for a moment to see what areas in your life have been affected because of anger, hate, and resentment. You are still harboring hate over something that happened to you a long time ago. There is no freedom to create, expand, and become who you were born to be.

    Take this time to forgive, forgive, and forgive your past. Bless and embrace your past. See all your past experiences as wisdom and teachers who were present so you could evolve to your next spiritual unfoldment. We are here to live our life purpose, to be happy, joyous, and prosperous and to share our gifts and talents with the world. Let's start the process of forgiveness and letting go of the past.

    On this next page, write down names of people you are still holding a grudge against and think about the experience that created all the disconnect between you and the person or experience. I am taking a stand for your greatness and salvation. Please don't overlook the simplicity of this exercise. Truly become present to all the emotions like anger, sadness, revenge, and hate, and express yourself in this book.

There is tremendous healing power in this book. Remember, you are not alone on this journey we call life. We are all in it together like brothers and sisters. Rejoice in this sacred moment of peace. I recommend listening to New Age music to create a safe place of receptivity and forgiveness. The music will raise your vibration frequency to love, peace, joy, forgiveness, harmony, and gratitude.

Take a deep breath, and set an intention for healing and love to take over your heart with this exercise. Go for it. I'm here cheering for you. Namaste.

Chapter 12

Love, Forgiveness, and Gratitude

As I come to the end of my book, I want to touch upon the power of love, forgiveness, and gratitude. I like to refer to them as "the positive trio." Where one is, the other two are right around the corner, which is great because the more love we have in our heart, the easier it is to forgive and then rest in gratitude. You see, God, spirit, and omnipotent presence are made up of unconditional love. We all come from this beautiful energy called love. We are all love, regardless of all the injustices done to us. If you strip away someone's upbringing, what's left is love. Even though my brother molested me when I was six years old, I never stopped loving him, especially now that he has made his transition into the spiritual realm. As this book is coming to its fruition, so is my brother's salvation. I believe that, even though I never had the chance to express my hurt from his betrayal, now his soul can rest in peace. That's the power behind love, forgiveness, and gratitude. I am grateful for this opportunity to put this secret to rest.

You see, whatever secret you have been concealing, my dear spiritual warrior, now is the time to set yourself free from the bondage and chains of the past. Use my story as your gateway to confront, address, and make amends with the childhood abuse in your past. I assure you that life will never be the same again for you, which is a good thing. Start to let go of your shame, guilt, and anger, and allow the positive trio to transform and heal your life. Open your heart to heal your past wounds. Now you have a choice to tell a new story. No matter what stage of awakening you are currently at right now, start the process of letting go of all the garbage that has been preventing you from living your dreams. Your past will continue to haunt you as long as you give it permission to do so. Let's stay connected to the positive trio and allow them to change your heart and attitude and liberate yourself from the past. The more love keeps showing up in your life, the easier it is to forgive yourself for all your mistakes and injustices done to you. Forgiving is an ongoing process of dropping the ego, embracing your spirit, and being grateful for everything in your life.

Now some of my readers might get annoyed with me about my forgiveness attitude, but if it weren't for forgiveness and love for myself, I would not be sharing my story with the world. I first had to forgive myself and everything about my past in order to release the poison inside of me. Once I started implementing the positive trio in my life, I was able to be at peace with myself and accept myself wholeheartedly.

Jesus said that we must forgive seventy times seven. Matthew 18:21–22 says, "Then came Peter and said to him, Lord how oft shall my brother sin against me, and I forgive him? Until seven times; but, until seventy times seven."

Why is forgiveness so important in someone's life? As you can see, to forgive seventy times seven seems unreal and almost impossible to do. It's easy to say you are a spiritual person, go to church, pray, and meditate, but if something traumatic happens to you, then it's not so easy to do.

Remember this, my spiritual warrior. True spirituality is when we practice the principles even though we don't want to go through the emotions and changes in our life. It was not easy to forgive my sexual abuse, but I needed to set myself free from my past. So I started practicing the spiritual principles that I have been sharing throughout my book so you can start doing the same.

Let's say that, until now, your past has been haunting you for over ten years. You experienced some form of childhood abuse, and you kept blaming your failure on your past. I know this might sound harsh or upsetting, but it's time to face the truth about what is. The past happened, it was unpleasant, things were done to you, and life just didn't make sense.

Okay, let's walk through the door of forgiveness today. These five stages are only possible by you practicing forgiveness seventy times seven. That means the ego takes over your language and behavior when you have any opportunity to do something wrong. You stop, pause, and ask for forgiveness right away. It is better to love than hate. It is much better to get along than to be distanced and isolated from your friends and family.

Everyone is trying the best he/ she can with what they have at this moment. No one is perfect, and we are all bound to mess up royally sometime or another. Let go of the judgment and harsh criticism, and heal yourself first. Practice humility, patience, kindness, acceptance, love, forgiveness, and gratitude. The world needs our help, spiritual warriors. The change only occurs in the world by us changing ourselves. Give yourself this gift of honoring your divine creation and life according to these spiritual principles that are here to help us live in alignment with our soul's purpose in life. You are an amazingly beautiful person. God adores you, and He is happy you are reading my book. This book contains intense healing, light, and power to set yourself free from your past. Trust your intuition, and continue on this journey to the brand-new you.

This is your season, my dear friend. I honor your existence, and your desire to read my book humbles me. I wrote this book for you. In order to set myself free from my past, I had to do something of service. I want you to live happy with no more drama and tears from your past. It is time to rejoice and open the treasure that lives inside of you. Knowing that my story will make a significant difference in someone's life, gives me great joy. Take my story, and be inspired to share your story about your challenges and triumphs. You are a spiritual warrior. You are capable of doing anything you put your mind to.

When God created us, He was smiling and pleased with His creation to the world. Start doing things you always dream about doing like traveling, starting a new business, going back to school, and making a commitment to have an extraordinary relationship with your soul mate. Life is waiting for you to tell it exactly what you want. Don't be shy or vague about your desires and wants. God placed them in your heart because He wants to give it to you. If you believe you don't deserve good and plenty, then that's exactly what you will get. It has been a long journey to heal from the past and see yourself as this brand-new you.

How did you get here? What events transpired that led you to reading my book? This is synchronicity that started the chains of events to coincide with your desires. You attracted this book into your hand. That's how the universe operates on your behalf. It supports your desires the moment you set an intention for something new to happen in your life. I'm excited for you and can't wait to hear your story of transformation and reinvention to the brand-new you.

This leaves us with the best part of the book, gratitude. What are you grateful for, my spiritual warrior? Have you allowed yourself to tap into this immense, powerful force of the universe called gratitude? Think about everything you are grateful and thankful for, and dwell in that sacred space of light, possibilities, and freedom. Gratitude is a feeling of appreciation or thanks. It is the state of being grateful and thankful. Gratitude is the key to open the abundance and prosperity in your life.

This emotion or feeling state is where magic starts to take over your being. If we don't honor and appreciate what we have now, then how do we expect the universe to give us more if we don't treasure what we have now? Let's say that you are tired, broke, and homeless with nowhere to go. All of a sudden, someone extends his/her home to you, food to eat, clothes to wear, and a family that will support and love you as its own. This might sound far-fetched, but this happens many times in people's lives.

If we are expecting good things, good things will come to us. If we don't value ourselves, then the universe will do the same. I could remember many times in these past two years where I couldn't pay my bills or rent on time. I decided right there and then to practice gratitude, and everything worked out to my favor. Money showed up from everywhere—clients and friends—and I was able to live my life in peace and gratitude. It is very easy to talk about gratitude when everything is going well, but the challenge is when you are down on your luck and nothing seems to be working out for you. You know what I'm referring to. You just broke up with someone, your physical health is down the toilet, and your car broke down after you paid a couple thousands of dollars to get it fixed. That's when gratitude is the only thing you have, and it's free.

The space of gratitude connects you to God. You start to feel better about your life even though the circumstances are still the same. The reason is that gratitude, even though intangible, lives in the spiritual realm of possibilities. That energy only attracts more of the good that you want in your life.

As I end my book, I have so much gratitude in my heart that it's a true miracle this book has manifested in my life. I am blessed to have beautiful people in my life, and I thank God for choosing me to bring this message to the masses. I love my family, and I only have the deepest gratitude in my heart for them. I am free to live my life with freedom, purpose, and truth. That is what I stand for in this world. I thank you for reading my book and sharing my journey with me. I know in my heart that your life will change forever. I bid you farewell, and may God's blessing be bestowed on all your desires. Namaste.

Conclusion

As I look back at my journey, I appreciate how wonderful God is in my life. The path to awaken to the brand-new you takes courage, discipline, determination, self-love, and a willingness that never stops. All the examples I openly shared about my life are to allow you to see where you have fallen short from manifesting all you can be. This path is for those who are sick and tired of living a lie and pretending to be someone they are not. Once that decision is made to change your ways, then the universe opens the doors to unlimited possibilities. All the tools are now available at your disposal. From here, you move forward, closer to the radiant light that powerfully lives inside of you. Take my story, and share it with your friends and family so it can give you something to fall back on. Use my story to see into what has been preventing you from releasing your true potential. I believe we all have a unique story to share with the world, one of struggles, challenges, and triumphs that make us who we are today.

Living your truth for the first time will feel awkward and weird in your mind and body. That's okay. Some memories from our past will bring up strong emotions. The key is to use those past experiences and notice how they have prevented you from truly shining your light. This is a great segue into what I have noticed recently about why I have been playing a small game in my life.

When I was in the fifth grade, I was pretty well known as one of the fastest kids in my school. Running came easily for me, and I loved to play tag and all the running games that were popular in that era. To my delight, I was chosen to represent my school's relay running team to compete with the other schools in our district. Keep in mind that I was a shy boy who really had low self-esteem and no clue what I was supposed to do in the race. Because I was the fastest on my team, my coach designated me as the anchor for the race.

Come race day, I can vividly remember how nervous and anxious I was, questioning my ability to remember what to do and hoping I didn't screw things up for our team. As you can imagine, what we think about, we bring into our life experiences through our thoughts and strong emotions. When my team player passed the baton to me, I dropped it.

Let's replay this critical moment in slow-motion time so you really get the blessing from my story. The moment I dropped the baton, life stopped. I could hear people screaming in the stands and my coach telling me to pick up the baton, run, and finish the race. That experience, which I'm pretty sure was about ten to fifteen seconds long, felt like an eternity. I was embarrassed, disappointed, overwhelmed, and sad, really not knowing what to do next. Finally, I picked up the baton and finished the race, making our team last.

That experience has been buried deep in my subconscious mind all the years until now. Because of that experience, I decided that I would not put myself out there again to feel and experience those negative emotions. This was a way of protecting myself and playing small and safe in my world. The fascinating discovery about this story is, "How can a child determine to never try his best from that experience?" This is an interesting question I want you to ask yourself.

I know we all have experiences that we'd rather not face or even think about because it just makes us feel bad. The truth is that those experiences that happen in our childhood bring tremendous awareness and freedom once we clear up that energy in our body and our subconscious mind. The subconscious mind is the inventory of our life. The mind does not care whether the experience brought you joy or shame. It only responds to how connected we are to our emotions that determine the experience of being real and concrete.

Here's the good news. Your negative experience came bearing gifts for you to grow and expand into the brand-new you. What we can't accept about our life will eventually control and dictate our destiny. We have an opportunity today to recall that experience and learn from it. Notice if you experience any discomfort in your body. We tend to store our experiences in our body as a way of dealing with it or not.

In yoga, as you start going deeper into your practice, you will have moments when that memory will become real in your body, and you have a tool to work through it with your poses and breath. This is really important for you to get now. When you awaken to the brand-new you, that means you are releasing all negative thoughts, emotions, and experiences that no longer serve your highest good.

Jesus said, "And no one puts new wine into old wineskins. For the wine would burst the wineskins, and the wine and the skins would both be lost. New wine calls for new wineskins" (Mark 2:22). What that biblical verse translates to is that, when our emotions, habits, thinking, and behaviors change, we must start fresh and not from the old self. You cannot add something new from an old consciousness. You must be willing to release the old and embrace the new. Whatever took place last year is no longer relevant to what is happening now in this moment. Starting from a new place gives us freedom from the past. Your old wineskin must be discarded in order for new life to emerge from you.

Sometimes, we want to suppress all our defeats, mistakes, struggles, and negative emotions deep in our subconscious mind so we can start anew. Once our awareness and consciousness expand, now we are ready to pour new wine into our new skin. The new wineskin is your consciousness, and the wine is your brand-new you.

Take full inventory of your life today. What is missing and why? What deep desires are churning inside of you? Is there something that you must accomplish before you die? Have you made your bucket list?

Think about those questions and write down your answers on the next page. Anytime we write things down, our awareness grows and expands to bring that thought into existence in our physical world. Remember, the more you get involved with this process of awakening to the brand-new you, the bigger your transformation would be.

Write down your bucket list and make one a reality.

The journey continues…

* * *

Welcome back, spiritual warrior. Thank you for being open and honest with yourself about what is missing in your life. I just want to share some final thoughts before we wrap up the show.

This life is a gift from God. He gave us life everlasting to fulfill our calling in life. No one has the authority to tell you how to live your life. Live your life from your heart, and pay attention to your intuition. Don't be afraid to make mistakes, fall on your face, or look stupid in front of people. We are here to be the best we can be with what we have. Don't give up on yourself so soon. Take time to finish each season as each comes to you. As we mature into who we are becoming, the change will be everlasting. Give yourself permission to see your goals through to the very end. Complete with what you have started, and try your best each day.

If it's weight loss, understand that you will be tested numerous times to solidify your commitment to being lean and healthy. There will be days that you want to eat everything in sight because you feel restricted with your food. It's okay. That's natural, and it will pass. The main thing is to never give up on yourself. Once we do that, life gives up on us.

I hope my story helps you see your life differently today. As I shared earlier, the struggle with my sexual abuse took a strong hold on my being. It felt like I was in prison for a long time. The addictions would resurface anytime I was ready to give up on me. This journey has not been easy for me to walk, yet I openly share with you my darkest secret that kept me in captivity from truly living my life's purpose. I am thankful that my journey was not in vain, and I pass the baton to you to run and win your race.

I give you my deepest gratitude and love for humanity. I wish you abundant blessings. May you start your journey today to awaken the brand-new you. Namaste. The light in me sees and acknowledges the light in you.

"As you become more clear about who you really are, you'll be better able to decide what is best for you - the first time around."

- Oprah Winfrey

Personal Notes

References

Addair, G. (2013, Sept 24).
    Cloture Club. Retrieved from http://www.clotureclub.com/2013/09/everything-want-side-fear-george-addair/

Addiction.(n.d.). In Merriam Webster Online, Retrieved August 23, 2014 from http://www.merriam-webster.com/dictionary/addiction.

Anderson, C. (2014, Aug 1). Survivors. Retrieved http://www.malesurvivor.org/survivors.html

Chemicalization (n.d.) In Truth Unity Retrieved from http://www.truthunity.net/texts/rw chemicalization

Child abuse. (n.d.) In Child Abuse Definitions, Retrieved August 23,2014, from http://www.childhelp.org/page/-/pdfs/Child-Abuse-Definitions.pdf.

Hicks, A. (2014, Aug 1). In an excerpt from a workshop July 8, 2000. Retrieved from http://www.abraham-hicks.com/lawofattractionsource/index.php

W., B. (n.d.). Alcoholics Anonymous. Retrieved from http://www.aa.org/pages/en_US

James Dillet Freeman's poem, Prayer for Protection. Used with permission of Unity, www.unity.org